West Swindon

Composite aerial photograph of most of West Swindon taken in 1995

West Swindon

WHAT THE EYE DOESN'T SEE

Angela Atkinson
Frances Bevan
Roger Ogle

HOBNOB PRESS

First published in the United Kingdom in 2023
by The Hobnob Press,
8 Lock Warehouse, Severn Road, Gloucester GL1 2GA
www.hobnobpress.co.uk

© Angela Atkinson, Frances Bevan, Roger Ogle, text and images, 2023

The Authors hereby assert their moral rights to be identified as the Authors of the Work.

All rights reserved. No part of this publication may be reproduced, stored in a retrieval system, or transmitted in any form or by any means, electronic, mechanical, photocopying, recording or otherwise, without the prior permission of the publisher and copyright holder.

British Library Cataloguing in Publication Data
A catalogue record for this book is available from the British Library

ISBN 978-1-914407-57-4

Typeset in Chaparral Pro, 11/14 pt
Typesetting and origination by John Chandler

Front Cover: Looking over West Swindon in 2003. The Spectrum/Renault building is in the foreground, with the since demolished Westlea Campus behind it. The Link Centre and Shaw Ridge Leisure Park are in the centre. In the distance is Freshbrook and the Blagrove employment area.

Back cover: West Swindon is renowned for the collection of public sculptures described in this book. This image shows a fleeting, artistic installation by young people who saw creative possibilities in the heavy snowfall of January 2010

CONTENTS

	Preface	6
1	The Beginning of the Western Expansion	9
2	The Street Names	25
3	Before the Beginning	32
4	Open Spaces and Public Art	37
5	Lydiard House and Estate	63
6	St Mary's Church	75
7	The Farms of West Swindon	82
8	The Twentieth-Century Buildings	108
	And to End	150
	Acknowledgements	152
	Index	153

Preface

THIS BOOK started out as a list of twenty-five buildings for inclusion in a photographic record of the area by Angela Atkinson and Roger Ogle.

Yet it soon became clear that the West Swindon we know today has stories to tell. It is almost sixty years since policy makers and planners turned their attention to how and where the town's expansion might next take place. But before considering that, it's useful to explore first the area's history so that we can put the modern surroundings into context.

The area has notable Roman history, even prehistory, and this book gives a flavour of that. It also, thanks to years of painstaking research by Frances Bevan, tells the stories of the farms of the Lydiard Estate and the house and the church.

From Barbury Castle's Hill, West Swindon sits sparkling
A mix of buildings and trees stands proudly
A thumb-shaped print on the Wiltshire map
Of criss-cross lines old and new

A community of friends
Waiting for the break of dawn
The first light of a new day
The first signs, sights and sounds of morning
Waking, yawning, stretching,
Like a slow-motion movie.'

Students from Greendown Community School and local primary schools worked with their teachers and poet /animator Marcus Moore to produce almost 700 lyrical lines known as *Westwords*. This all happened across a six-month period through 1997 and 1998.

The poem enjoyed one performance at the 1998 Swindon Festival of Literature but wasn't ever published or recorded. In 2018, some of the young people involved twenty years earlier worked with current Lydiard Park Academy students to commemorate the cultural journey in space and time and verse, with contributions from parents and teachers.

The full poem was then published for the first time. An abridged version of Westwords can be viewed at https://vimeo.com/267986921.

The Westwords poets with their teachers in early 1998

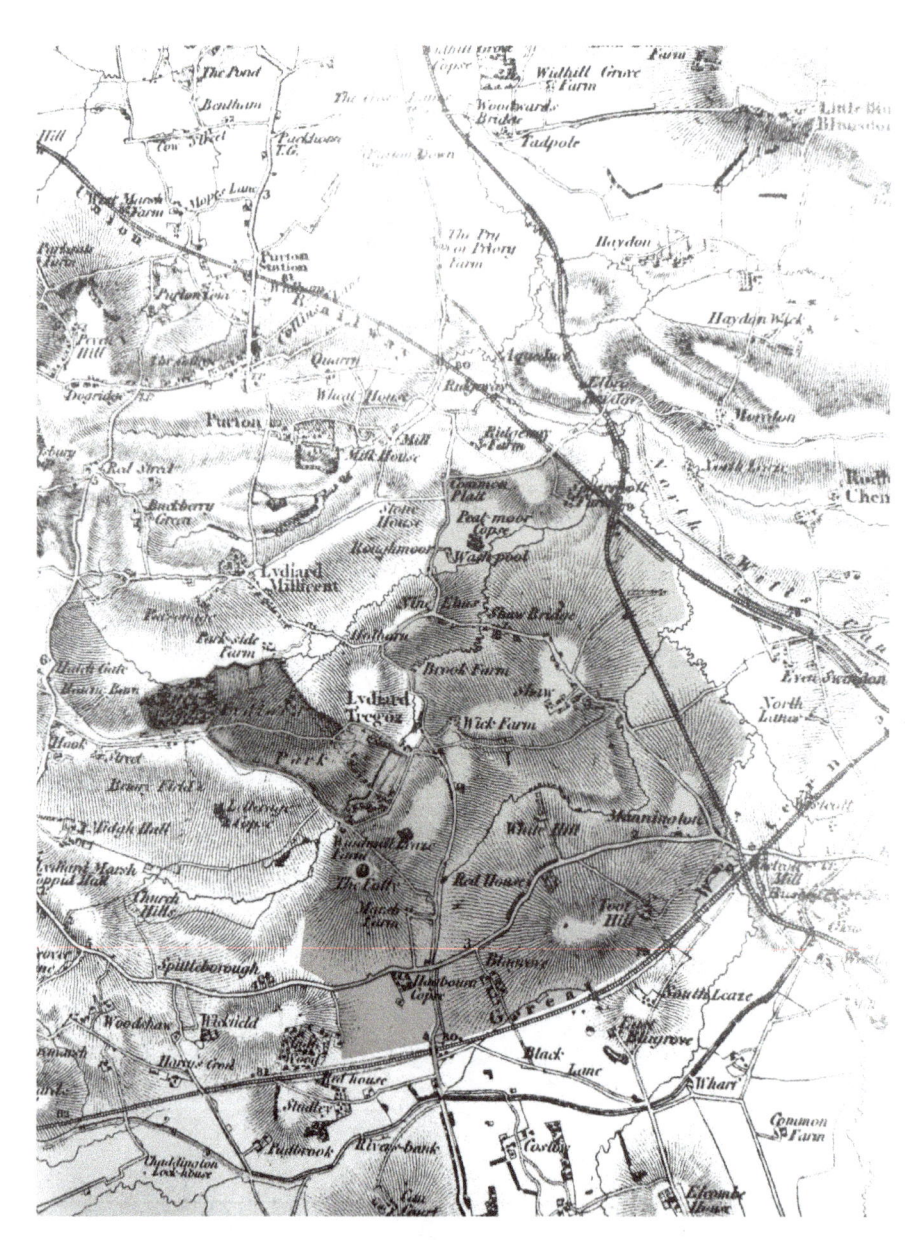

A 19th-century map of the land west of Swindon, with the town's western expansion shaded in grey

1
The Beginning of the Western Expansion

the start of an emerging city in all but name

ROGER OGLE

Until the early 19th century the road from London to Bristol, to the west of the small hilltop market town of Swindon, was the scene of most activity in a tranquil area. The land between the River Ray and Lydiard Park comprised low hills and farmed fields. Meanwhile the hamlet of Shaw lay on the route between Swindon and Purton. The tenants of Lord Bolingbroke at his country seat at Lydiard House occupied most of the farms. Many would have attended the 13th-century St Mary's Church, built next to the original front entrance to the big house.

Here then existed a quiet, evolving, environment for several hundred years. Yet the needs of the expanding population across the country and the poor transport infrastructure needed investment in the means of carrying goods in bulk. In the late 1700s and early 1800s there came the digging of the Wilts and Berks Canal, to the south of the high place named Toothill. Soon after came the North Wilts Canal, close to the River Ray, built as a north–south link to the River Severn.

The rapid industrialisation of Britain and the development of railways had a more profound effect on Swindon. Founded in 1833, an August 1835 act of Parliament incorporated the Great Western Railway Company. The company bought land. Then the young engineer, Isambard Kingdom Brunel, surveyed the route from London to Bristol. The line was built in sections and trains started to run to the south of Toothill

The past and the future. Taken from Toothill, the beginning of the demolition of Swindon's railway works in the early 1990s

Farm in 1841, close to the canal that carried the coal required by the steam engines.

The year before, Brunel and Daniel Gooch, the GWR locomotive superintendent, and later company chairman, identified the area below the hilltop town – the halfway point between London and Bristol – as suitable for an engine maintenance centre serving the west of England. Within a short time, the Works became a locomotive and rolling stock design and manufacturing plant. It rapidly became the largest employer in the town.

The railway works stimulated every aspect of the regional economy. Not least here was the demand for construction labour to meet the urgent provision of housing. It continued to shape the development of Swindon for more than 120 years. The Works dominated the town until the end of World War II. Yet the expansion of the road transport network and the opening of new industries made it clear that continued reliance on the railways comprised a danger to the local economy. This was the beginning of another transformation of Swindon's economic and social structure – one that saw the town become more integrated with the world economy. Companies from the USA, Europe and Japan arrived

WHAT THE EYE DOESN'T SEE

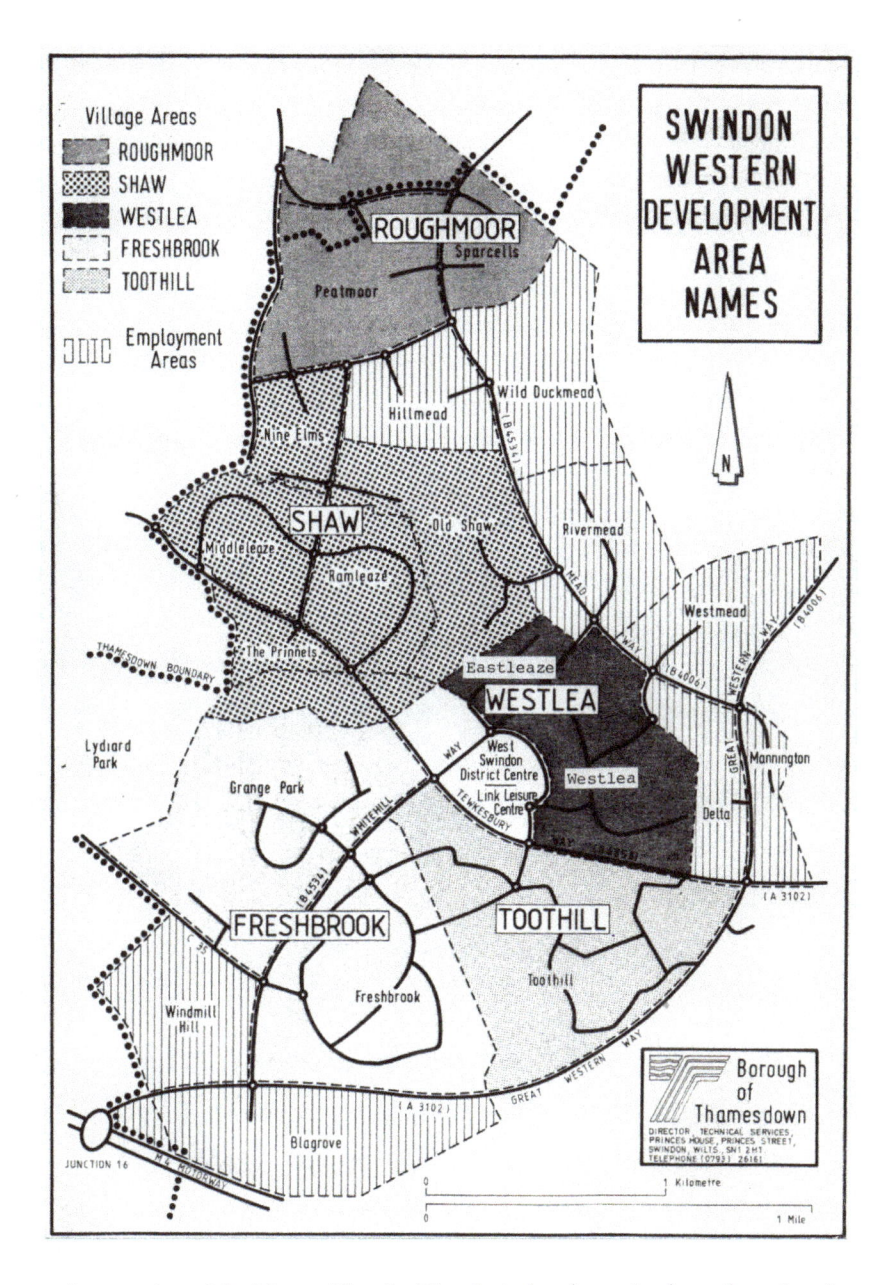

An overview of the Master Plan for West Swindon drawn in the early 1980s. It should be noted that Wild Duckmead was identified for employment in the very long term, after the former landfill site had been stablised. It was later designated as public open space. Also, the part of Roughmoor north of Purton Road was denied planning permission and remained in Wiltshire

with investments and job opportunities in manufacturing, electronics, computer technology and information-based services.

As with the arrival of the railways, a need for more housing, educational, leisure and commercial facilities accompanied this employment growth. Development across farm fields had taken place in every direction around the town and, by the 1960s, the borough council was pushing for more expansion. This was later incorporated into a central government regional plan which considered sites for a new city to the west of London in West Berkshire or North Wiltshire. With Newbury being too close to the capital, Swindon found itself identified as the most suitable town for expansion. Population growth projections suggested that the town should grow from some 100,000 in 1961 to become a city of 250,000 by 1981. Then, perhaps, 400,000 by the year 2000.

Swindon Borough Council's enthusiastic interest in expansion and its track record of growth saw planners from Swindon, Wiltshire

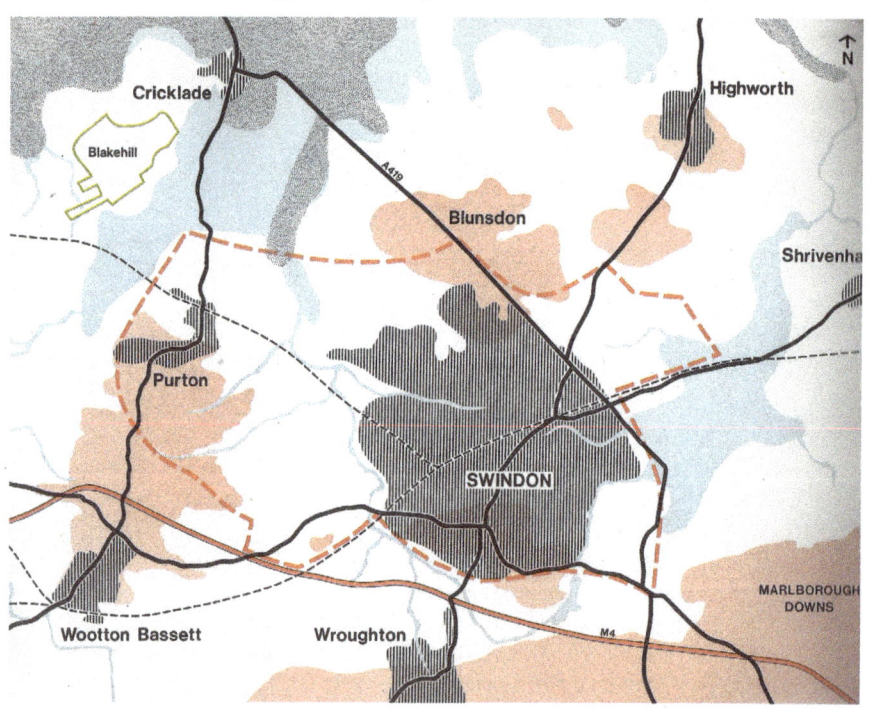

The illustration from the 1968 report 'Swindon: a study for further expansion' - the Silver Book. The red line shows the extent of the expansion envisaged for the town

A model photographed in the Silver Book showing a proposed district centre close to Mouldon Hill

County and the Greater London Council collaborate on a report published in 1968. It set out how and where it might be best to achieve such growth. *Swindon: a study for further expansion*, known as the 'Silver Book' (after its shiny cover), identified vast extensions beyond the existing urban area. The proposed expansion covered land east of Stratton St Margaret, north of Haydon Wick and westwards beyond Rodbourne. The boundary to the west took in Lydiard Millicent, Purton and halfway to Cricklade.

Central government scaled back the original population target to around 250,000 souls by the end of the century, a figure that comprised 75,000 incomers and natural population reproduction.

The Silver Book provided the principles of development around the idea of the 'urban village'. These, the report proposed, would comprise 5,000 to 8,000 residents focused on a local centre. Each centre would have shops, a primary school, a community centre, medical facilities and a church. The report identified local open spaces close to housing as an important need.

It envisaged a larger district centre offering a varied range of larger shops and recreational facilities. The document includes illustrations of such a centre close to Mouldon Hill. That plan had leisure facilities around a lake large enough for sailing boats fed by the River Ray.

A 'better social balance' was a key objective, to be achieved by a mix of local authority and owner-occupied housing. Based on the experience of earlier town expansion, social development was a concern alongside employment opportunities. The report recommended the employment of community development workers to welcome new arrivals and help the formation of local groups in community centres.

Initial expansion based on the Silver Book principles took place to the east at Liden and Eldene. As implementation for the plans for these areas took place, attention turned to a much larger development westwards. This was set out in a further report by planners from Swindon, Wiltshire and the consultants who authored the Silver Book. This much shorter technical document, published in 1971, gained the moniker of the Gold Report, again after the colour of the cover. It disregarded the borough's boundary at the time to identify possible development sites to the west and north of the town which were, in the main, within Wiltshire.

Planners identified two areas for the next stage of expansion. One, to the south of Shaw Ridge between Mannington and Blagrove, is now covered by Toothill, Freshbrook, Westlea, Eastleaze and Grange Park. The other was to the north of Haydon Wick. That's the location of Abbey Meads. Groundwell Ridge and Priory Vale which was eventually built in the 1990s and 2000s.

Being closer to the town centre and existing areas of employment, as well as the recently completed M4, the first option found favour. But the planners determined the need for a new road to the M4. The new suburb was to be by-passed by the Great Western Way to the south of Toothill, and the old Swindon to Bristol A420 became incorporated into the new housing area.

Wiltshire County Council, with planners from Swindon and central government, took part in drawing up the Silver Book. Indeed, the county sold 580 acres of land to Swindon for the first phase of the western expansion. Yet it refused planning permission, believing the application to build 'to be premature.' Central government had to press for an overturning of the decision to meet the demand for housing. Thanks to that delay, 1974 arrived before work on the first infrastructure began.

In the initial phase south of Shaw Ridge, the borough master plan for Toothill and Freshbrook set out a mix of local authority and private housing. The development at Westlea, Grange Park and Eastleaze required engagement by the majority land owner E H Bradley Ltd. They planned for almost exclusively private housing. The company also part-owned the site earmarked for the West Swindon District Centre. It meant modification of the Silver Book principles as Bradley's argued that Westlea didn't need a village centre. Their reasoning being that the District Centre would provide for residents' needs.

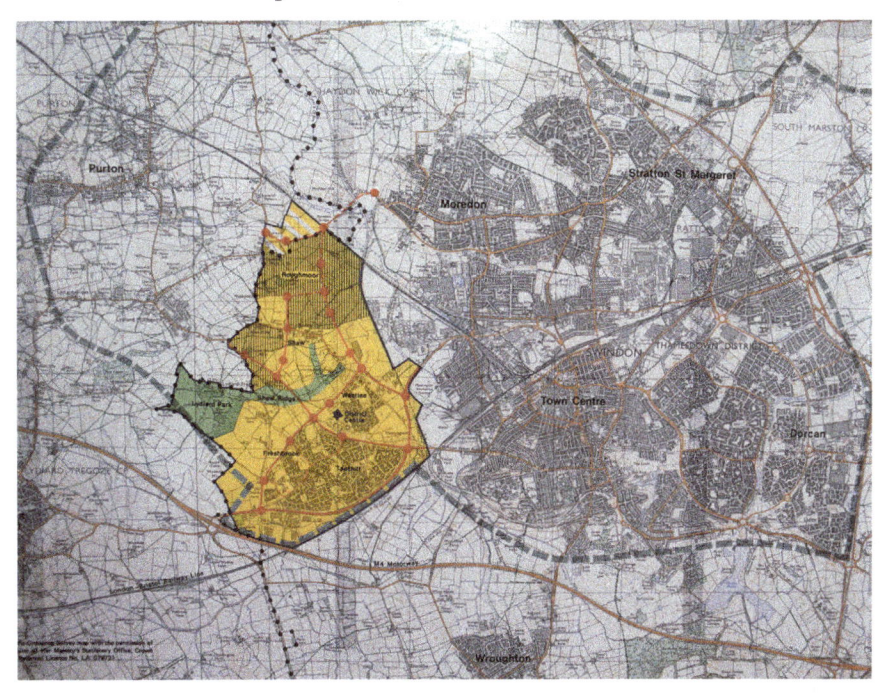

The boundaries of the Western Expansion area proposed by Swindon Borough Council in the 1971 Gold Report taking in Ridgeway Farm (the yellow and white striped area)

In 1977 the next phase of development to the north of Shaw Ridge required another master plan application. The borough council drew this up in consultation with the major landowner, Wimpey, and a consortium of house builders. Again, Wiltshire County Council, supported by North Wilts District Council, local parish councils and the original Shaw Residents' Association, objected to another major expansion. This area would become Shaw, Ramleaze, Middleleaze, The Prinnells, Nine Elms, Peatmoor and Sparcells. After a planning enquiry, the Department of Environment granted permission for the development to proceed.

It's interesting to note that the master plan included housing development, with a village centre, north of Purton Road at Ridgeway Farm. The planning inspector excluded this area from the plan. This forced relocation of the village centre to the south overlooking Peatmoor Lagoon at Roughmoor – the composite name for Peatmoor and Sparcells.

Thirty-five years later there came a reversal of that decision. In 2012 a planning inspector rejected objections from Wiltshire Council, Purton Parish Council and Shaw Residents' Association to building at Ridgeway Farm. They accepted landowner Taylor Wimpey's argument that housing in Wiltshire, was, to all intents and purposes in Swindon. The company had to allocate land for a primary school, but sites for shopping or community facilities were not provided.

Going back to the early days of the 'western expansion', the first people started to arrive at the end of March 1976. After a move to Penhill broke down, Terry and Theresa Davies were the first residents of a small group of houses at Markenfield beyond Mannington roundabout.

1976: the Mayor of Swindon Percy Jefferies presenting a commemorative spoon to Terry and Theresa Davies and their baby Janice, the first born in West Swindon (Swindon Advertiser)

WHAT THE EYE DOESN'T SEE

It was a sea of mud served by a bus stop half a mile away. With Theresa expecting their first child, the couple soon moved in. Baby Janice was born a few weeks later, the first of many to be born or move in with their parents over the coming years.

1977: the temporary shop and community hall on Dunwich Drive, Toothill (Swindon Advertiser). Below, the hut became an arts workshop in 1979 where sculptors in residence created some of the public artworks on show across West Swindon

This was the beginning of a period of rapid development, with well over 1,000 houses built each year between 1979 and 1989 across the town. Each year 800 houses went up in West Swindon during this period. A mobile shop served the first residents, with social meetings taking place in one of the new houses. In 1977 came the provision of a builders' hut on Deerhurst Way, Toothill. Half of it served as a cramped and damp shop, the other half was a social hall. Meanwhile, four new houses opposite were converted into use as a health centre.

Whilst the Silver Book and various other reports set out theoretical principles for policy makers and planners to follow, the human dimension to the western expansion demanded flexibility in delivery. The rocketing population had expectations for social facilities. These expectations put pressure on the new councillors elected after the area transferred from Wiltshire to Swindon in 1981.

Toothill Church and a permanent shop arrived in the village centre in 1977. And 1978 saw a primary school built close by. Toothill Farmhouse and its barn underwent conversion for community use, but it was away from the centre of the community. In April 1983 a public meeting, held in Toothill Church, discussed the building of a large multi-purpose sports facility with a library, arts and community spaces. At length this facility became known as the Link Centre. The event soon turned fractious, with residents demanding the promised community centres at Toothill and Freshbrook. By then housebuilding at the latter was fast taking place. People said they'd waited long enough. They feared the proposed leisure centre would mean their local needs would get forgotten. The development managers had to rethink the timing of local provision. In a short time they agreed funding for community buildings at Toothill, Freshbrook and Westlea at Upper Shaw Farm.

Despite the frustrations of residents with Swindon, some services such as education, youth work, social services and highways remained with the county until Swindon became a unitary authority in 1997. In the early years the population comprised a high number of young couples of child-bearing age. Despite Wiltshire County Council's objections to the expansion, the education authority had the legal obligation to build schools.

At first children of all ages in Toothill needed bussing to Park South, before Toothill Primary opened. Oliver Tomkins Church Aided

WHAT THE EYE DOESN'T SEE

Windmill Hill Primary School opened in a semi-permanent building in Autumn 1987 to relieve the pressure on Freshbrook primary. The demand decreased when Tregoze primary opened in Grange Park in 1991. As part of schools reorganisation Windmill Hill closed in 2007 and combined with Freshbrook to become Millbrook Primary. The land on which it stands was originally designated for housing. In 2023 it remained unused.

Infant and Junior schools, and schools at Freshbrook and Westlea soon followed. For a time, Freshbrook Primary was the largest in the country. It had some 1,000 children accommodated in permanent and temporary buildings. Relief to that situation came when Windmill Hill Primary School opened close by in a semi-permanent building.

The granting of permission for expansion north of Shaw Ridge, saw primaries built at Shaw Ridge between Eastleaze and Ramleaze. Then Tregoze in Grange Park, Salt Way in Middleleaze, Brook Field in Shaw, and Peatmoor at Roughmoor Village Centre.

With so many children growing up in the area, it became necessary to bus the youngsters to the Ridgeway secondary school in Wroughton

In 1986, to mark the tenth anniversary of the first residents arriving in West Swindon. I organised an exhibition of photographs of community life alongside a display by the Borough of Thamesdown's town planning department explaining how the expansion to the west of the town came about. As West Swindon approaches it's fiftieth anniversary, this book is a successor to that event.
Pictured, the Mayor of Thamesdown Harry Garrett at the launch evening with many of the people who moved into the area from March 1976.

and Bradon Forest in Purton. At length, Wiltshire agreed to build a secondary school, Greendown Community School in Grange Park. The first children arrived in September 1986 and Princess Anne performed the school's official opening the following April. The policy was to start a new year group over the following six years. This meant the continuation of bussing children out of the area for several years.

By the mid-2000s, the number of primary-age children had dropped. Thus, Swindon Borough Council (the education authority from 1997 when responsibility transferred from Wiltshire) came under funding pressure from central government to reduce the number of school places. Windmill Hill merged with Freshbrook, which was rebuilt. Meanwhile Salt Way combined with Shaw Ridge in a new building on an adjacent site designated, in the first instance, for a Roman Catholic primary. Secondary-age children were able to access out-of-area schools, as long as parents funded their transport. In 2012 Greendown underwent rebranding to become Lydiard Park Academy and received permission to open a sixth form.

The turn of the millennium saw most of the planned 11,500 homes completed. The population of the town had increased by 25,000 to 30,000. West Swindon has continued to grow beyond the original master plan with new sites receiving planning permission. In the early 21st century more houses appeared off Hook Street and at Ridgeway Farm in Wiltshire. Meanwhile the former employment area at Westlea Campus gained a new use, finding itself replaced by a supermarket and houses.

As the Community Development Officer from 1979 to 1990, for Thamesdown Borough Council (Swindon's local authority between 1974 and 1997), it was clear to me that calling the area the 'Western Expansion' was not tenable in the long term. I was also involved in the foundation of the *Link* magazine - distributed to every house free of charge. From the start, the designation West Swindon was used to describe the fast-growing, geographically distinct locality. It was a way to help residents identify and build community spirit with the wider district within the town. It also helped with putting down roots in the 'village' that they were living in. It was certainly uncomfortable to live in the expansion area for the first few years – unsurprising, given that it was a huge, muddy, building site with few facilities. There was a great deal of negative publicity across the town in that early period, often emphasised by the local press. This was the central issue that *Link* magazine set out to tackle, doing so by promoting community communication about all the good things taking place.

Perceptions changed within a few years. In particular after the West Swindon District Centre – the first out-of-town shopping complex with free parking – opened. The Link Centre with its ice rink and other facilities already mentioned, Shaw Ridge Leisure Park, and the maturing green environment made the area attractive to live in. Having lived in the area since I arrived in 1979, I concluded long ago that West Swindon is an appealing, positive and successful place.

Even the Russians took an interest

A fascinating collection of maps held in Swindon Central Library illustrates how Swindon was of interest to the USSR after World War II until 1989 when the Berlin Wall fell, followed by the collapse of the Soviet bloc.

During the Cold War period, when the threat of nuclear destruction was an ever-present worry, Russian map-makers were busy translating maps of Britain into Cyrillic type. Why they did this isn't clear so far as Swindon is concerned. The close proximity of three strategic RAF air bases at Lyneham, Fairford and Brize Norton, and other military installations nearby, meant that Swindon was vulnerable to radioactive fall-out.

The maps were updated from time to time as the images show. The map of Swindon and its surrounds does not include the westward growth of the town. But a later version includes the first phase of the western development and shows Toothill, Freshbrook, parts of Westlea, including the West Swindon Centre, but not Link Centre.

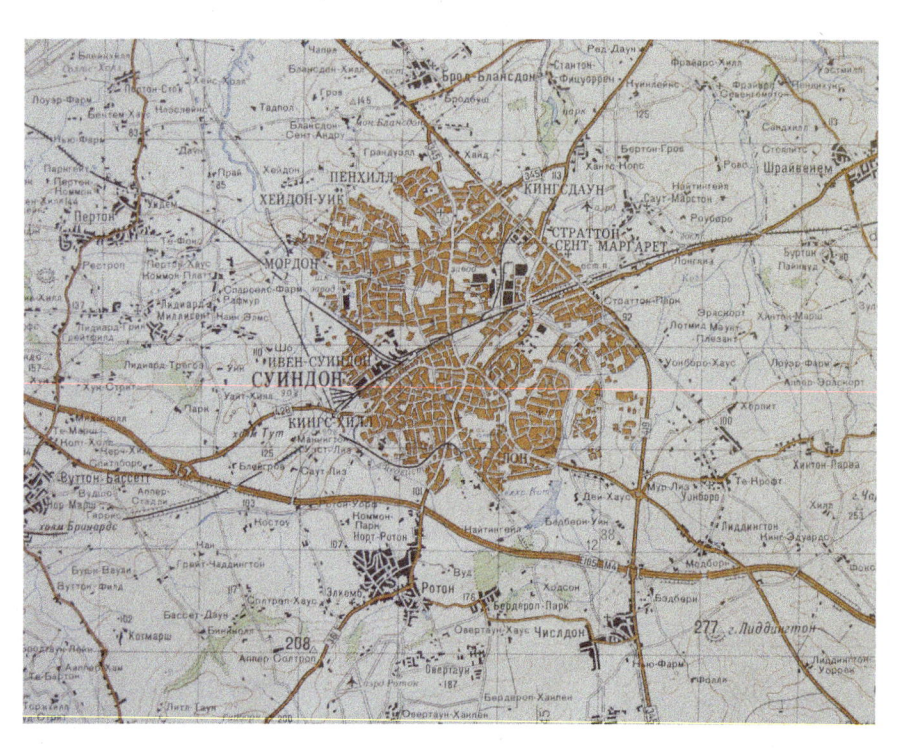

водоочист. ст.
ферма Лоуэр-Шо
ферма Аппер-Шо
107.0
93.0
92.0
спорт. пл.
шк
спорт.пл.
зона отдыха
Маннингтон
УЭСТЛИ
МАННИНГТОН
94.0
96.0
лесп.
спорт. пл.
шк
ТУТХИЛЛ
99.0
125.0
101.0
коттеджи Саут-Лиз
Саут-Лиз

The road west in the early 1970s. The A420 Wootton Bassett Road meeting the under-construction Great Western Way at Mannington (Swindon Advertiser)

2
West Swindon – Street Names

Frances Bevan

ALLOCATING STREET NAMES to the vast new West Swindon area may sound an engaging exercise. Yet it wasn't without its problems, as the Thamesdown Borough Council records (1983-1988) reveal. The council was the street naming authority. They worked in consultation with the Post Office and the developers, with an approved list of names circulating between the three bodies. But things didn't always go according to plan.

The western expansion, which began in 1975, would, in the first instance, include four urban villages. A predicted 25,000 residents would fill these villages. And all would have a myriad of roads, streets, closes and cul-de-sacs in need of identification.

This development was first known by development site numbers. Then came working titles and marketing names adopted by the house builders for advertising. Some areas were soon identified by the use of existing farm names such as Toothill, Shaw and Mannington. Roughmoor Way leading to Peatmoor takes its name from a former farm. The area of Peatmoor was an ancient tract of low, marshy ground. Here saw the building of the lagoon adjacent to Peatmoor Copse. That is a surviving fragment of Bradon Forest, which once covered North Wiltshire. Sparcells Drive lies upon the site of Sparcell's Farm, while Ridgeway Farm sits at the northern end of our patch, across the Swindon boundary, in Purton. This was at first proposed for inclusion in the expansion. But a planning enquiry, in the early 1980s, blocked that plan.

The four arterial roads around and though the western development are the A3102, B4006, B4553, and the B4534. The A3102, the Great Western Way, extends from the M4 Junction 16 to Gorse Hill and the Transfer Bridges. The B4553, the main road from the town centre through the development, gets its name, Tewkesbury Way, from an ancient town lying to the north-west in north Gloucestershire. It was the site of a medieval abbey and a bloody battle during the War of the Roses. Fought on 4 May 1471 the Battle of Tewkesbury secured the throne for the Yorkist Edward IV in a significant victory over the Lancastrians. The B4534 became Whitehill Way. It got its name from a farm once owned by the governors of Charterhouse. While the B4006 became Mead Way, a common field name found on several farms in the Lydiard parishes.

1978: starter homes being built at Conisborough in Toothill

Toothill was the first area to welcome the new residents. The name Toothill, marks an ancient meeting place set on a piece of high ground. From it early occupants could see and defend the surrounding countryside. Thus, we have the selection of a medieval naming theme for this area. The first families moved into Markenfield in March 1976, a road named after a moated manor in Yorkshire dating from the 14th century.

Edington Close, off Beaumaris Road, took its name from a Wiltshire village with a 14th-century church. But this also had a much older history. Edington was the site of a great battle in 878 when King Alfred led an army of warriors against the marauding Danes.

Street names in Freshbrook continued the medieval theme, adding in another battle or two. The Battle of Stamford Bridge took place in 1066. Thus, it lends its name to Stamford Close near the Toothill roundabout. Meanwhile Wakefield Close commemorates the Battle of Wakefield, a skirmish that took place during the War of the Roses in 1460. Rowton Heath Way begins at the Freshbrook Roundabout and snakes its way through Freshbrook to Beaumaris Road. This road takes its name from the Battle of Rowton Heath. That conflict took place on 24 September 1645 during the English Civil Wars.

Houses fronting on to Idovers Drive, Toothill, looking out over Wiltshire

The third area of development, Westlea Down, comprised Westlea and parts of Grange Park. Landowners Bradley led this section, with its central feature of the West Swindon Centre including superstore, leisure centre and library. In 1981 Bristol builders Barrett were working on the 'Highgrove Area 4B Westlea Down.' Then, in December 1981, McLean Homes confirmed their choice of street names as Applewood Court, Littlecote Close and Fox Wood.

By 1983 work was under way in an area then referred to as 'Greendown Park, Area 8C1, Westlea Down.' A rather terse letter arrived at Thamesdown Borough Council, signed by D.H. Sacof of the Standard Housing Company. The letter requested information required for the production of a sales brochure.

> It would be a great help, if you could at least advise us of the choice of road names that might be available both for the main road through the site and the five cul-de-sacs.

The advertising name for Area 7B2 in Grange Park was 'Lydiard Chase' while McLean Homes advertised area 71 in Shaw as 'Maple Heights'. In 1984, Lydiard Millicent Parish Council expressed concern over the advertising name 'Lydiard Green' chosen by developers for another area of Grange Park. Both the Parish Council and Thamesdown Borough Council felt concern that there would be confusion between the new development in Grange Park and the existing area in the parish of Lydiard Millicent. The contractors were, therefore, requested to 'refrain from referring to the name Lydiard Green as much as possible in an attempt to reduce the risk of any confusion'.

Residents of The Holbeins in Grange Park taking part in a community tidy-up in 2008

In 1988 development of Grange Park continued apace. In Area 6E, Barrett Bristol Ltd was advertising homes in 'Oak Meadows', where street names Marney Road, Gerard Walk and Rycote Close received approval. Close by, in Area 59, a Tudor theme continued with Holinshed Place named after Raphael Holinshed. In 1577 he published an influential history of England, Scotland and Ireland. Sudeley Way takes the name of Sudeley Castle in Gloucestershire. It is advertised as one of the best Tudor castles in England and the burial place of Henry VIII's last wife, Katherine Parr. The road is part of the Holbeins housing development, named after Hans Holbein, the Tudor court artist, famous for his portraits of the King and several of his wives.

1980s: The farm fields off Hook Street, before house building commenced in Grange Park. The Cornflower pub at Freshbrook Village Centre can be seen in the distance

When it came to naming the agricultural-themed Ramleaze, the Post Office rejected a broad selection of the names on offer. So, Cotswold, Dorset, Jacob, Portland, Ryeland, Southdown, Suffolk Swaledale, Guernsey, Sussex, Dales, Exmoor, Coveney Medway, Wyndham, Brecon and Saxony all got the thumbs down. At length everyone settled on Hampshire Close, Alpine Close, Highland Close, Stanbridge

A brief moment in the early 1980s when the future by-passed the past, when traffic still used the section of Hay Lane between Hook Street and Grange Park Way, just before the completion of Whitehill Way. The old and new road signage can be seen, with the Cornflower pub at Freshbrook Village Centre in the background

Park, Charolais Drive, Shetland Close, Redcap Gardens and Berkshire Drive for Area 77 Ramleaze. The Post Office also objected to the use of 'Middleleaze Drive' and 'Ramleaze Drive'. They felt they would lead to confusion, but they remained unaltered.

As development in Shaw continued, the main theme of agricultural history became supplemented with a sub-theme of influential people in agriculture. This included Gabriel Plattes – a 17th century writer on agriculture and science. And Michael Menzies – who, in the 18th century, invented and patented a machine to thresh grain. Also William Winlaw, who invented and patented many new agricultural machines and pieces of equipment during the 18th century.

In 1985 Clarke Homes (Avon) Ltd received notification of the approval of Clarke Drive, Baird Close and Cartwright Way as street names and postal addresses for Area 72, Old Shaw, although Cartwright Way would later find itself changed to Cartwright Drive.

Development began on fields at Wick Farm in The Prinnells area in the 1990s. Once part of Viscount Bolingbroke's Lydiard estate, the names of the closes overlooking Lydiard Park took inspiration from the St. John family. Spencer Close takes its name from Lady Diana Spencer. Not the modern-day Diana but the daughter of Charles 3rd Duke of Marlborough and the wife of Frederick St John 2nd Viscount Bolingbroke. Lady Diana shared an ancestry with the late Diana, Princess of Wales.

Walter Close takes its name from Sir Walter St John. And Wilmot Close after his nephew John Wilmot 2nd Earl of Rochester, poet, libertine and friend of Charles II.

The street naming project of the 1970s, 80s and 90s, with the inclusion of medieval references and farm and field names, has contributed to preserving the history of West Swindon's ancient past.

You can discover the story of the naming of West Swindon's streets on a collection of microfilm reels held in Local Studies, Swindon Central Library.

3
Before the Beginning

ANGELA ATKINSON

WAY BEFORE EVER town planning consultants wrote the Silver Book described in Chapter 1, and even before the rich stories from the farms of the Lydiard estate, there existed here pre-Roman and Roman life. The definitive account, from prehistory to the recent past, you can find in *The Archaeology of the Borough of Swindon*, by the late Bernard Phillips. All we can hope to do with this volume is give you a few tantalizing titbits, enough to give you the sense of how the present is built upon the past. Bernard identifies in his book, pottery finds and middle- to late-iron-age artefacts. These artefacts indicate small settlements at Toothill Farm, Upper Shaw Farm and Ridgeway Farm.

Clive and Amanda Heard from Peatmoor examining building post holes excavated at Ridgeway Farm in 2011. The posts would have supported an Iron Age dwelling somewhere between 750BC and the coming of the Romans in AD43. They were discovered during the archaeology survey which preceded housing development

Artist's impression of the Roman kilns at Whitehill (Alison Borthwick)

Though most of Swindon's Roman activity took place on the town's east side, around Ermin Street, there are fascinating glimpses of it here in the west. There's evidence of enough wealth in the area to buy items imported from across the Roman Empire. Such artefacts included vessels from France and foods from Italy and Spain. On what's now Kiln Park in Toothill, once Whitehill Farm, there existed a Roman pottery. We know this thanks to the discovery of pottery fragments along with locally-made jewellery, furniture and household items. On this park there grows a tree, encircled with terracotta tiles commemorating the existence of the Roman pottery.

The Romans had a policy of working with local leaders and encouraging them to take on the trappings of Roman society. Findings of terracotta tiles, pottery and a walled cemetery indicate the presence of a villa at Reid's Piece in Purton. During the development of North Swindon, well documented excavations and ground radar surveys in the mid-90s and early 2000s revealed, at Groundwell Ridge, a villa, other significant buildings and terraced areas, and pools relating to the cult of Isis.

Bernard's book tells us that contemporary documentary evidence identifies the existence of a large medieval village at Lydiard Tregoz. That said, pointers to its exact location are few. It's feasible that it lay in the vicinity of the existing church and original manor house. Various digs and cable laying to the houses in the western expansion uncovered many pottery fragments. But the best guess is that the remains of the village

The scene at the archaeological dig for a Roman villa at Groundwell Ridge in North Swindon in 2004

lie beneath the large field at the west end of Shaw Ridge, outside the present park boundary, adjacent to Hay Lane.

Following the relative calm of Roman times, the centuries following their departure were riven with invasion and conflict as regional kings made alliances or fought each other for supremacy. One major historical event was the Battle of Ellandun in September 825. Where exactly it took place is unclear. Some say it took place near Wroughton, others believe that the armies of Wessex and Mercia clashed to the west of Lydiard Park. But wherever it was, it was without mercy: a brutal and bloody battle.

Henry of Huntingdon's Norman chronicle writes: 'the brook (*rivus*) of Ellandune [*sic*] ran red with gore, stood dammed with battle-wreck, and grew foul with mouldering corpses'.

Local researcher Graham Philpot supports the West Swindon location.

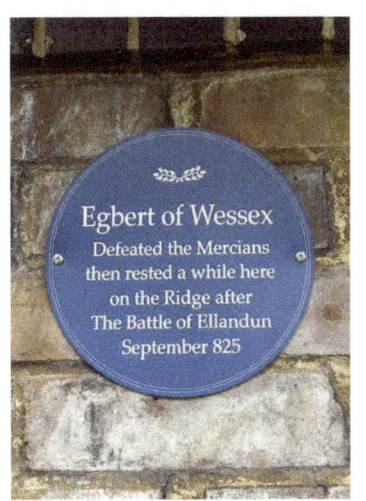

Plaque mounted at the entrance to the Bramptons housing development on Shaw Ridge – sadly vandalised shortly after it appeared

> A likely scenario for the battle would have the current position of Lydiard House as the Mercian army's starting point. The Wessex forces approached from the south west and formed on the high ground at Marsh Farm (now Windmill hill) to the south of the park. The stream that runs through present day Park Farm and Lydiard Park may be the brook choked with corpses mentioned by Henry of Huntingdon. The Lydiard location is favoured, in my view, because primary sources mentioned mounted forces and the fact that Saxon commanders preferred deploying along ridges before battle commenced.

The victory at Ellandun secured the predominance of Wessex and laid the foundation for Alfred and his grandson Æthelstan to create the nation of England.

His descendant Harold tried to protect the consolidated borders of the country north and south, but William of Normandy eventually defeated him at the Battle of Hastings in 1066.

The Norman conquest saw the imposition of a feudal order, whereby William's supporters from Normandy imposed a new feudal regime. They and some English backers became the predominant landowners, with tenant farmers and peasants paying homage and rent to them.

This era started the shaping of West Swindon in terms of the landscape and the construction of notable buildings such as the manor house that preceded Lydiard House and the adjacent St. Mary's church.

4
Open Spaces and Public Art

Roger Ogle

Green open spaces

West Swindon, as a large urban housing area, boasts an impressive amount of green space and tree cover, with a network of footpaths linking them together. These features attract people to live here and many choose to stay to put down roots.

The scene was set in the 1968 report *Swindon: a study for further expansion* – the Silver Book. It stated: 'In the future there'll be mounting demand for increased recreation and leisure time activities.' It explained that the demand would come about by the rapid expansion and the increasing spending power, leisure time and mobility available to present and future inhabitants. The report referred to the provision of playing fields and the need to preserve elements of the agricultural past. It called for a network of open spaces, as well as significant tree planting to supplement and replace field hedgerows lost to development. Large scale planting to establish new woodlands was advised, particularly on

In the 1980s the borough council's landscape department was imaginative in the overall look of open spaces, particularly in the striking annual display of daffodils. Unfortunately, they weren't maintained. Spring is Sprung facing Great Western Way has disappeared under mature trees. Swing into Spring, overlooking Tewkesbury Way was mowed into oblivion.

The 'fort' play area between Turnham Green and Worsley Road, Freshbrook in the early 1980s. Although it was exciting for youngsters, parents complained about railway sleepers which oozed tar in hot weather

Another popular play area built in the 1980s was Eastleaze Fields, next to Shaw Ridge Primary School. Most of the original play equipment was replaced as it wore out over the years

skylines to provide a strong background to such major urban features as industry, roads and motorways.

We can thank Swindon's urban planners and an influential team of landscape architects of the past for implementing the principles set out in the report. They decided to preserve as many of the old field boundaries defined by hedgerows and to plant trees in abundance.

Type a postcode into the Know your Place website (https://maps.bristol.gov.uk/kyp/?edition=wilts) and you'll see a side-by-side comparison showing the layout of the modern development and how it used the landscape.

Local open spaces, with a range of formal play equipment suitable for different age groups were given strategic locations between housing developments. The borough council was able to determine points of provision for open spaces and play areas in the first phase of expansion at Toothill and Freshbrook.

The pattern was set and followed for areas where private developers were the land owners. There are now twenty local open spaces across the area, maintained by West Swindon Parish Council. Two no longer exist, at Corton Crescent, Westlea and the other close to Shaw Village Centre which has been built upon. In more recent times the parish has funded a skate park and a cycling pump track off Westmead Drive.

Four larger areas of environmental importance bear deeper examination. In the past, the level of tree cover across Britain was much, much higher than it is today. Wood was a vital material for all aspects of life – building, agriculture, shipbuilding and of course fuel. West Swindon, before the agricultural revolution in the 17th century, would have comprised a patchwork of woodland, copses and small cultivated fields. But the increasing population and the migration of people to towns led to changes in farming techniques and far greater food production. This meant draining land and clearing woods to create larger fields.

The thriving pottery industry at Kiln Park, established during the Roman period, depended on managed areas of coppiced hazel to fuel the kilns.

Peatmoor Copse
It is not known if the Romans had any involvement in the woodland to the north of West Swindon. But the few records that exist suggest that

Peatmoor Copse, an ancient feature now surrounded by housing on three sides and Peatmoor Lagoon to the east

the 6.5-acre wood could be a fragment of the ancient Bradon Forest, it once being a 13th-century royal hunting ground that covered much of North Wiltshire. In those day a forest would have comprised extensive woodlands, scrubland and cultivated fields suitable for a wide range of animal and birdlife.

The period between the 15th and 19th centuries saw land cleared for agriculture. People living here then kept the copse to provide wood for fencing and fuel and also willow for local basket weaving needs. There's no evidence of building there thanks to unusually wet ground conditions. Whereas most of West Swindon has been built on clay, the copse grows on an underlying strata of coral rag rock which keeps rainwater close to the surface. Thus, we have the damp ground.

With only farm tracks around the area making it difficult to transport trees to sawmills, the wood fell into disuse from the early 20th century. The new availability of less labour intensive and cheaper materials for agriculture, construction and fuel also contributed.

The master plan for Swindon's growth westwards in the 1970s recognised the importance of protecting the copse as a rare example of a wet woodland, both as part of the flood mitigation strategy and also as an environmental corridor incorporating the newly-created Peatmoor Lagoon. In 1988 Swindon Borough Council brought together a group of volunteers to manage the copse in the traditional way. The emphasis now is looking after the ecology of the site and maintaining an educational amenity.

The woodland is divided into compartments, with trees cut using hand tools to allow light into dark areas to encourage wildflowers, insects and birdlife. Those caring for the copse create different environments each year, as the trees regenerate over the coppicing cycle. About a quarter of the copse gets left untouched to allow nature to take its course.

The health of the planet is high on the public agenda, particularly around finding ways to reduce carbon dioxide in the atmosphere. A wet woodland that's never undergone cultivation nor had buildings on it, its soil comprises several metres of accumulated organic material. Hence it acts as a carbon sink trapping CO_2. Although the ancient woodland covers six and a half acres, new tree planting around it since the late 1980s makes the total about ten acres. Peatmoor Community Woodland is a tiny element in mitigating climate change, but an important one locally. Find out more at: https://peatmoorcopse.mystrikingly.com.

Peatmoor Lagoon

The West Swindon master plan for the area north of Shaw Ridge determined the need for a large rainwater storage area. Its purpose was to reduce flooding downstream on the River Ray and River Thames. The lagoon was built on water meadows between two streams, Shaw Brook draining the farm fields to the west and Lydiard Brook flowing from the park. They met close to the boundary of the copse where 19th-century

Peatmoor Lagoon nearing completion in 1987, before Mead Way, opened, left, just as building works on the Chinese Experience restaurant started

maps show a sluice gate to regulate the amount of water flowing into the meadow.

The planners could have left the existing depression in the landscape to become a marsh at times of heavy rain. But engineers, landscape architects and ecologists worked together to design the ten-acre lake capable of storing up to thirteen million gallons of water. A weir with several shelves at the eastern end regulates the volume of water flowing away. Large numbers of trees and shrubs were planted on the banks and two islands. In the main this is all left unmanaged.

Footpaths surround the lagoon to create a pleasant environment for visitors, wildlife and birdlife. A gravel beach created on the northern edge allowed for the launching of model boats and feeding waterfowl. But from the start, the design included fishing platforms with the lagoon stocked with fish from Coate Water Country Park.

Hagbourne Copse

Tucked away in the corner of Blagrove industrial estate is a remarkable survivor of West Swindon's rural past. Hagbourne Copse is an area of approximately five acres managed by the Wiltshire Wildlife Trust. The

Peatmoor Lagoon, looking west towards Peatmoor Copse and the farm fields beyond Swindon

contrast between the noise and rush from the major roads and the calm of walking around the mature oak trees in the copse couldn't be starker. Famous for its magnificent spring display of bluebells, the copse is home to a diverse flora and fauna including more than five species of butterflies.

Hagbourne Copse appears on 18th-century maps and was, in all likelihood, planted before 1766, although it could be much older than this. On the tithe apportionment map surveyed in 1841, it forms part of more than 108 acres of woodland owned by Viscount Bolingbroke.

Shaw Ridge Linear Park

The West Swindon master plan designated the high ground between the earlier and later parts of development as a linear park between the hamlet of Shaw and the entrance to Lydiard Park. Previously, the land was fields separated by hedges and single ancient oaks. But influenced by the Silver Book principles, developers planted thousands of

Bluebells in Hagbourne Copse

Shaw Ridge in the distance before the trees grew, looking south-east towards Upper Shaw Farm

trees which have increased the height of the area.

Since 2010 a group of volunteers have managed the new woodlands, clearing fallen branches and trees, building pathways through the woods and planting wildflowers on the edges and in glades.

Shaw Forest Park

Until the mid-1940s Shaw Farm supplied the town with milk from its cows and vegetables from its market garden. Wiltshire County Council owned the site and it became the rubbish tip for domestic and commercial waste until the mid-1980s. That period saw the installation of a series of leachate drains followed, in 1994, by a gas ventilation system.

The area was incorporated into the master plan for the development westward as a major open space. Compression of the rubbish from the expanding population, capped by clay, raised the

June 2004, residents mass against a proposal to turn Shaw Forest Park into a sporting hub

ground level across the ninety-acre site by about thirty-metres. This meant a great deal of landscaping to create a varied environment of flat spaces and hills. The soil used came from the housebuilding areas across West Swindon and from the excavation of Peatmoor Lagoon. By using a variety of methods to enrich the depleted soils, trees and vegetation were given the best chance to survive. From the air it is possible to make out the figure of Gaia, the goddess of the earth in the landform.

Tree planting at Shaw Community Forest started in 1993, with two events involving hundreds of Swindon families. The Chinese Experience restaurant sponsored the first, in 1995, as it coincided with Chinese New Year.

But the park's future came under threat in 2002. A commercial developer proposed the site as a large sporting hub, including a new stadium for Swindon Town Football Club. Public protests soon forced site owner Swindon Borough Council to block any further consideration. As a result, a third, celebratory, tree plant took place in 2003. In between these engagements, the bulk of the tree planting was undertaken in phases by contractors. Tree planting was largely completed in 2004. That said, 2018 saw some small open areas planted as climate change mitigation.

Today a large proportion of the ninety-eight acres are accessible,

Community tree planting at Shaw Forest Park, 1985 to mark Chinese New Year in 2001. The Mayor and Mayoress of Swindon David and Jenny Cox took part with local families

with about a quarter of the land used for solar panels and closed to the public.

River Ray Environmental Area

The Midland and South Western Junction Railway, a north–south route from Cheltenham to Andover, linked to other railways serving the Midlands and the south coast. The first section opened in 1883 and closed to passengers in 1961, though some goods services continued to 1970.

The route skirts West Swindon. With the River Ray it forms a physical separation of the expansion area from the town. In 1978 a group of volunteer enthusiasts formed the Swindon and Cricklade Railway Preservation Society, their mission being to reconstruct and preserve a section of line. The restored line runs for 2.5 miles from Mouldon Hill Park almost to Cricklade.

The section adjacent to West Swindon, running between the artificial hills of Shaw Forest Park, became the River Ray Parkway. This is an eight-mile walking and cycling route from Mouldon Hill to Old Town. It's also an environmental attraction with several notable features. Close to Sparcells, it's possible to visit a section of the former North Wilts Canal and its towpath. Further, a tunnel under Thamesdown Drive is ready for use if plans by the Wilts & Berks Canal Trust to link the waterway to the renovated canal south of Toothill at Wichelstowe are ever achieved. Along the River Ray Parkway to the south, the Wiltshire Wildlife Trust is involved with three environmental projects.

Swindon lagoons bird and wildlife sanctuary lies at the northern end of the Thames Water Barnfield sewage treatment works, opened in 1884. Until 1985, in addition to treatment of sewage, fifteen ponds of different sizes were in use as storage for waste products from industry around the town.

Due to modern waste treatment technology needing less land, and to meet environmental improvement legislation, most of the ponds had a clean-up and planting took place.

Swindon Lagoons wildlife sanctuary, from the closed part of Shaw Forest Park

Additionally, two shallow lakes were created with the specific purpose of attracting migrating birds and wading waterfowl. Under the management of the wildlife trust, volunteers maintain a range of habitats and ensure that the open water doesn't turn into woodland.

Because of the deep water in some of the ponds, as well as the uncertain ground off designated footpaths, the area is not open to the public except on supervised open days. Thanks to its closure for generations, it now hosts a huge variety of wildlife. Find out more and take a virtual tour at www.wiltshirewildlife.org/swindon-lagoons-swindon.

2005: Wiltshire Wildlife Trust project officer Jo Sayer at the newly completed meandering of the River Ray at the Westlea to Barnfield bridge in the background

Further south at Rivermead, the River Ray had been straightened into a canal in the 19th century. In 2005 it was re-engineered back to its original meandering course to allow for better flood-water retention and improved habitats.

Next to the river, Rivermead volunteers created a community nature reserve. They planted and now maintain trees on mounds constructed from the spoil produced by excavation of the river basin.

Also, at the southern end of the River Ray Parkway is a recent project. It's a collaboration between the Wildlife Trust, Swindon Borough Council, parish councils and local community groups. The West Swindon section, between Rivermead Drive and the Western Flyer pedestrian and cycle route into the town centre, concentrates on flood mitigation from Westlea stream that flows into the River Ray. New flood storage areas take rainwater flowing through the housing areas upstream. While the planting of trees and creation of ponds attract birds and wildlife.

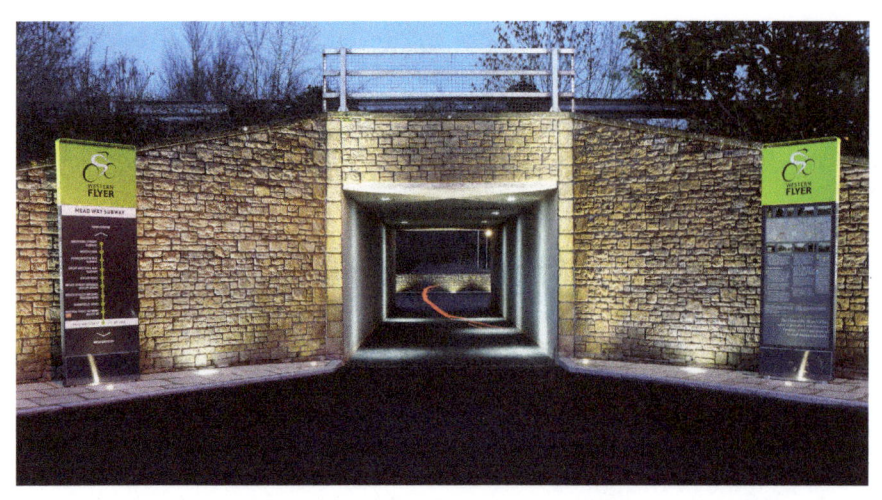

In the mid-2000s, the open spaces of the west were made more accessible with the creation of the Western Flyer, a two-mile cycle and pedestrian route which significantly improved road free travel to and from the town centre. The Swindon Travel Choices project starts at the Chesters Play Area in Westlea

Public art in the landscape

What makes West Swindon so unusual is the placing of sculptures throughout the area. They stand like above-ground archaeology, obvious yet unexplained, brooding in the landscape and surprising to the passer-by. Yet in this largely forgotten state, the art pieces add a certain mystery to the community.

Commissioned by Thamesdown Borough Council (Swindon by another name) in the late 1980s and early 1990s, they were funded by developer contributions and grants from charitable foundations. They're an important and unique part of the

Carleton Attwood with the Mayor of Swindon Mike Bawden at the unveiling of The Watchers in 1982. (Richard Wintle, Calyx Multimedia)

town's cultural make-up and deserve better recognition than they have.

1. *The Watchers, 1982, by Carleton Attwood (1908–1985) at Toothill Village Centre.* The first sculpture in West Swindon, cast in ferro-concrete at Swindon's town hall studios, is one of Carleton's last works. Due to his ill-health, sculptor Pat Elmore did most of the completion work. The work represents the guardians of the new community.

Looking to the Future sculpture installed in its original site at Westlea Park in 1985

2. *Looking to the Future, 1985, by Jon Buck.* Three enigmatic concrete and fibreglass figures in bathing suits rest by the ponds at West Swindon Centre. Jon Buck was the first artist in residence in West Swindon and created the figures in a temporary workshop in Toothill. They were first unveiled in Westlea Park but were later relocated due to vandalism.

The second unveiling by Mayor Jim Cordon on 1 May 1989 was

May Day 1989, Mayor Jim Cordon with Jon Buck viewing the sculpture relocated to the West Swindon Centre sponsored by the West Swindon Centre and featured the burying of a time capsule to be opened in 2089. It contains letters from young people, a tape of hit songs and details of a three-bed semi for sale at £75,000.

Jon Buck talks about his work before the sculpture was unveiled in Westlea in 1985 (https://vimeo.com/4381203?ref=em-share).

Hideo Furuta with his recently completed Nexus at Freshbrook Village Centre

3. *Nexus, 1986, by Hideo Furuta (1949–2007).* The late Japanese sculptor spent six months on site at Freshbrook Village Centre hand carving huge blocks of blue pennant stone – the same as used at Stonehenge – into three interlocking segments mounted on old railway sleepers. They're a massive presence within a busy urban setting.

Swindon Borough Council has replaced the wooden supports twice since the 1986 installation, in 2012 (partial) and again in 2023.

4. *White Horse Pacified, 1987, by Julie Livesey.* This imposing abstract concrete and metal structure sits in the bowl of a former quarry opposite the junction between Worlidge Drive and Cartwright Drive. It's an interpretation of the famous chalk white horses found across Wiltshire and close by at Uffington in Oxfordshire. It's the only 3D version and as such doesn't get the recognition it deserves.

WHAT THE EYE DOESN'T SEE

53

White Horse Pacified soon after unveiling. Note, in the background, the embankment supporting Mead Way in the background where drivers could view the sculpture

Sculptor Julie Livesey with models of White Horse Pacified which she designed in the old shop building at Toothill which had been converted into a studio

5. *How the Mighty Fall, 1990, by Tim Sandys-Renton.* Here we have a powerful sculpture in aluminium and cast iron. Surrounded by a large green space overlooking Ramleaze, it's a thought-provoking comment on the industrial age whilst referencing the history of Roman settlement in the area.

The Mayor of Swindon Ken Savage in January unveiled How the Mighty Fall with sculptor Tim Sandys-Renton and council leader Tony Mayer

David Putnam and Diana's son, the late Jason Dors-Lake introducing his daughter Morgana Ruby to her grandmother. (Richard Wintle Calyx Mutimedia)

The human form is imprinted upon aeroplane wings, with feet imprinted on solid wheels as if ready to roll down the hill and take off. The sculptor said, 'it gives the impression that man could fly and travel at will, yet is rooted to the spot.'

6. *Diana Dors - Film Star, 1991, by John Clinch (1934–2001).* Film producer David Putnam and

WHAT THE EYE DOESN'T SEE   55

Diana's son Jason Dors-Lake, unveiled this flamboyant, larger than life portrait of the late, Swindon-born actor, Diana Dors. It's situated outside the cinema at Shaw Ridge Leisure Park.

7. *Hey Diddle Diddle, 1992, by Vega Bermejo.* Carved from Portland Stone, this charming lyrical sculpture sits close to the junction of Tregoze Way and Spencer Close at The Prinnells.

Hey Diddle Diddle by Vega Bermejo

Art in the community
Toothill Sunrise, 1985, by Keith Gale. When visiting the *The Watchers* sculpture at Toothill Village Centre, look through the doors of Toothill Community Centre. Located in the barrel roof you can see a stained-glass window unveiled soon after the building opened. It depicts the new urban development set in Wiltshire countryside, with references to Swindon's railway heritage and the high-tech future of the town.

The committee of residents preparing for the opening of the community centre selected the design by Keith Gale from thirty-five submissions by students of stained glass at Swansea School of Art.

Student designer Keith Gale installing Toothill Sunrise with Tim Lewis, tutor at the Welsh School of Architectural Glass

Back to Back. Photo: Duncan & Mandy Wood www.oodwooc.co.uk

WHAT THE EYE DOESN'T SEE

Back to Back, 1990, Nick Moore. The sculpture is located at the entrance to The Quadrant, Stonehill Green, Westlea, the former Swindon hub for telecoms company Alcatel. Weighing over nine tons, it shows three life-sized figures. One is naked, another wears a suit while the third is clad in overalls. Together they hold up a large bowl. Nick Moore described the piece as showing how we are all the same underneath. He further commented that the site, with its landscaping and attractive brick and glass building, suggested to him a parody of a classical fountain.

Alcatel – later Alcatel-Lucent – closed its Swindon operations in 2014. In 2020 the building was reopened as serviced apartments. Back to Back is now hidden behind new houses built next to Stonehill Green.

New Purton Road bridge, 2002. West and North Swindon were joined in December 2002 when a new road bridge was opened over the Swindon to

Sunrise over Purton Road Bridge

Gloucester railway line. It replaced the 19th-century single lane bridge which remains in place as a pedestrian and cycle route running parallel to the new road.

The £1.25 million engineering structure also became the town's largest work of public art, with the concrete parapets formed into a 40-metre-long frieze. The design by Richard Perry incorporates transport, industrial and environmental themes. The old bridge was the scene of tragedy in 1988 when Mark Hinton, twenty-eight, threw himself onto a train after strangling his partner Sarah Winrow, eighteen, at their home in Pinehurst. The inquest heard

Together with Gordon Dickinson, Mandeep Nahal, Lewis Harris, Rebecca Bissex, Max Read, Connor Moody, Louise Farndale

Princess Anne under the Westlea Primary School welcome arch when she visited the founders of the Story Sacks Project in 1998.

WHAT THE EYE DOESN'T SEE 59

that he was jealous and possessive of Sarah, especially after she showed interest in another man.

Together, 2003, Gordon Dickinson. The outdoor steel sculpture was unveiled outside Westlea School to mark its twentieth year. Atalya Atherton proposed the name for the work. Close-by is a wooden welcome arch at the school entrance, erected in 1993, the tenth anniversary. The Friends of Westlea School were involved in fund raising for *Together* and in 2020 were involved in supporting the refurbishment of the work by Gordon.

Confluence, 2006, Gordon Dickinson. The curved steel artwork decorated with small tiles was created to mark the amalgamation of Salt Way and Shaw Ridge Primary Schools. Confluence was situated for a few months at Salt Way before it closed. Initially it was painted red, the colours of both schools.

Children with Confluence in their last weeks at Salt Way Primary in Middleleaze, before they and the sculpture moved to Shaw Ridge School in September 2006

But the new building at Shaw Ridge has green window frames so the sculpture underwent repainting to match following its move to its new, permanent location.

20th Anniversary Mural. To mark twenty years of town twinning between Swindon and Ocotal, Nicaraguan artist Patricio Marin Munoz from Ocotal painted a mural depicting scenes from the town and his country.

His visit was sponsored by Swindon Ocotal Link, a charity established after a devastating hurricane destroyed large parts of the Central American country in 1998. Over the years members of the charity assisted with building houses, funding a nursery and a seniors' care home. Visits by people from both towns also took place.

The mural is mounted within Lydiard Park Academy and can be viewed by appointment when the school isn't in session.

Lost over the years
Sculptured wood in Lydiard Park

Thunderbird totem pole, 1989, Fergus Mercer. The two-legged structure was carved from fallen trees. With a name board Tarzan Trail, it formed the entrance to the park's original play area.

Lydiard Park Arch, 1990, Anthony Holloway The artwork was crafted from the wood of chestnut and lime trees felled in the storms of 1989. On one side were carved Lydiard House and scenes from people's busy lives. On the other there were animals, insects and plants.

Both structures lasted a few years before the wood weakened, necessitating their removal.

The Link Centre. Several artworks were situated high in the library entrance atrium before the 2014 refurbishment of the building, after Swindon Borough Council leased the building to sports and recreation charity GLL.

On one side was *Animal Fantasia by Claudine Dunger, 1987* and *Palimpsest of Species by Graham High, 1990.*

On the opposite wall was the 1990 Link mural by Kim Creighton and Carlyle Reedy, painted to mark the twinning of Swindon and Ocotal. In 2007 two young dancers Edenia Rivera and Marco Rugama from Ocotal spent three weeks in Swindon visiting and performing in schools and community groups.

5
Lydiard House and Estate

FRANCES BEVAN

LYDIARD HOUSE started life as a manorial building before it grew to become a substantial mansion. When viewed from the front, the present house appears to be a somewhat grand, 18th-century building. An inscription in the attic records that the house as built in 1743 by John Viscount St. John – died in 1748. He married Anne Furnese, a rich heiress:

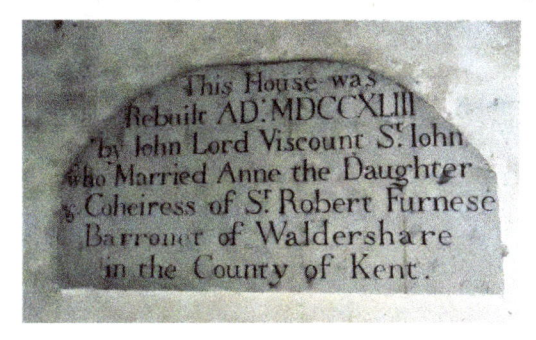

This House was Rebuilt AD:MDCCXLIII by John Lord Viscount St. John who Married Anne the Daughter & Coheiress of Sr. Robert Furnese, Baronet of Waldershare in the County of Kent.

In 1086 Alfred of Marlborough held the estate. But it wasn't long in passing to Harold, son of Ralph, Earl of Hereford. He gave Lydiard church to Gloucester Abbey in 1100. In 1256 the existence of a hunting park at Lydiard Tregoz is indicated by the king giving deer to restock it to the owner of the manor, Robert Tregoz, Sheriff of Wiltshire.

The coming of the Lydiard estate into the possession of the St. John (*Sinjin*) family intertwines with the endowment of the church to Harold, head of the Barony of Ewyas in 1100. From there it passed

Margaret Beauchamp, portrayed at the top of the St John family tree in the unusual polyptych in St Mary's Church, Lydiard Park

down the female line through subsequent marriages into the Tregoz, Grandison and Beauchamp families. There it remained until heiress Margaret Beauchamp married Oliver St. John in around 1425.

Grand designs

The beautifully restored Palladian mansion visitors see today is only part of the story of the history of Lydiard House. The property that survived the post-war cull of stately homes was the grand design of John, Viscount St. John. John used his wife's inheritance to remodel the St. John family country seat. The skeleton of that house lies within the 18th-century structure. The medieval property had a central hall block and screens passage with kitchen and solar wings to the west and east. (Screens passages were passage ways between the halls and service areas, and solar wings were the private, family rooms.)

John St. John, the aspirational 1st Baronet, carried out extensive alterations and enlargements during his 17th-century residency in the house. The 19th century saw the addition of a kitchen wing to the west of the property. But those aside, for over 250 years, Lydiard House stood in a state of benign neglect.

In 2021 the Friends of Lydiard Park commissioned a painting by local artist Billy Beaumont. Billy's painting depicts the house and gardens as it would have looked before John, Viscount St. John transformed the property and parkland. It is informed by a plan dated *c.*1700 that is held in an external repository.

Lydiard House, formal gardens and park. The contemporary illustration by Billy Beaumont. Image included with the consent of the Friends of Lydiard Park

So, how far back does the history of the Lydiard estate extend?

In 1270 Robert Tregoz received royal permission to enclose and impark a wood called Shortgrove to extend his deer park. But whether there was a house or hunting lodge in the grounds remains unknown. Perhaps even more intriguing was a discovery made during an archaeological investigation, in advance of the 2004-7 Lydiard Park Landscape Project. A trench dug in the area of the present church car park revealed reused Roman high-status materials. The findings included painted wall plaster, fragments of terracotta roof and heating tiles as well as pottery sourced from abroad. It is tempting to speculate on the Roman property that once stood in the vicinity of the present Lydiard House.

Lydiard House and St Mary's Church. (Darren Jack)

Today most of the former Lydiard estate farmland lies beneath the 1980s West Swindon development. But some of the last working farmers in Hook were the descendants of those Victorian tenants who doffed their caps and paid their dues to the St. John family at Lydiard Park.

Wartime service

During World War II the park served at various times as a prisoner of war camp, a transit camp for US soldiers on the way to

Nurses staffing the wartime hospital, lined up in front of huts that would later be converted into homes for Swindon families (Friends of Lydiard Park)

the D-Day landings, and a hospital for wounded soldiers.

Americans exploring the empty house left graffiti in its upper reaches. The post-war years saw the wartime camp buildings converted into temporary homes for Swindon families. One could say they were the first West Swindon community.

Flog it!

Parts of the once extensive 3,000-acre Lydiard estate went on sale in the 1920s. And in 1930 Mary St. John, Lady Bolingbroke, took the decision to sell off over 1,800 acres. The *North Wilts Herald* described it as 'one of the largest sales held in Swindon for many years.'

Lady Bolingbroke died in 1940 and two years later what remained of the estate went up for auction at the Corn Hall in Swindon's Cattle Market. The sale particulars of the remaining portion of the Lydiard Park estate included the historic mansion, pleasure and parklands, Windmill Leaze Farm, Creeches Farm, cottages and allotments. There were also several holdings of arable and pasture land, with the whole comprising approximately 750 acres.

In 1943, in the middle of World War II, Edward Hiscock, the sole surviving trustee of Lady Bolingbroke's will, decided to sell what remained of the Lydiard Estate. The gamble was a huge one, but the family had no option owing to the profligate behaviour of previous generations. By the 1940s the farms not already sold were mortgaged and the house was in a state of disrepair. In simple terms: the purse was empty. The emptiness of the St. John family coffers triggered a huge gamble by David Murray John, Swindon's visionary Town Clerk, to buy the dilapidated mansion. Uppermost in his consideration was the opportunity to use Lydiard House and park as a setting for further education.

It's fortunate that the recommendations made by John E.M. Macgregor, Technical Advisor, in September 1943 were not wholly embraced. In keeping with the idea to create a hostel and/or centre for further education, Macgregor suggested dividing the building. He opined the creation of

> a central lounge, dining rooms with cafeteria service, library, and two good recreation rooms in the fine architectural suite of the ground floor, with small boys' and girl's writing rooms at the extra ends.

The Drawing Room, Lydiard House, complete with St.John family portraits dating back to Elizabethan times and elements of original furnishings (Richard Wintle, Calyx Multimedia)

In 1955 the state rooms in Lydiard House opened to the public. And, in that same year, the house received a Grade I listing from Historic England. While the corporation set about recovering original furniture, fixtures and fittings, Lord Lansdown placed on loan furniture from Bowood House.

In 1958 Swindon Corporation and the Ministry of Works agreed upon a five-year period of restoration for Lydiard House. The Ministry would contribute £2,600 on an annual basis and the corporation £1,000 per year. In 1962 David Murray John submitted to the chairman and members of the development sub-committee a plan for the 'Restoration and Modernisation of Lydiard Park.'

As it happened, a plan already existed to convert the kitchen wing and upper floor as a conference centre. The Grade I listing recognised that the state rooms on the ground floor were of outstanding beauty, deserving of protection and opening to the public.

A hostel for young people with accommodation in the stables was soon up and running. Young people using the hostel facilities had to cater for themselves with simple camp cooking. By 1962 day conferences, meetings and, what was described as 'suitable social gatherings', were sometimes held in the mansion with guests employing outside caterers.

A mannequin of Lord Bolingbroke in his library in the late-1990s

Installation of a small, pre-fabricated open-air swimming pool came under discussion. The restoration of the long-silted up lake was of prime importance to Murray John with costs estimated at £9,320. This was only achieved in 2005. The proposals for the provision of the conference centre came in at an estimated cost of £24,470. These proposals included 'Adaptations, Equipment, Drainage Works, Reconstruction of Dam, Dredging of Lake, surfacing of road and the bathing pool. At the time of the report's writing, the corporation had already invested fifteen years of work to save Lydiard House and park for the use and enjoyment of Swindonians.

The Lydiard Park landscape restoration project saw the most extensive body of work take place on the Lydiard estate since Swindon Corporation bought it. Thus it completed the restoration plans begun in 1943. The Heritage Lottery Fund granted a £3.1 million award. Supported by RWE npower, Intel Corporation (UK) Ltd, BMW Group, English Heritage, DEFRA and Great Western Enterprise, it saw the restoration of 18th-century parkland features. The castellated dam wall,

Excavation of the upper lake at Lydiard Park in 2004

Visitors viewing the excavated plunge pool close to the lake

A horse team was employed to pull out overgrown trees cut down as part of the works to open up overgrown areas close to the lake

breached in the early 20th century, had repair works and the park saw reinstatement of the lost lake. Further, the works revealed a plunge pool, rediscovered during an archaeological investigation, and the state-of-the-art ice house underwent renovation. The walled garden underwent fresh laying out and planting to its original 18th-century plan before opening to the public.

Lydiard House and St. Mary's Church both received a Grade I listing in 1955. The park and garden received a Grade II listing on the Register of Parks and Gardens of Special Historic Interest in 1987, with a 2013 amendment by Historic England. The reason for designation is as follows: 'The park forms a strong group with its associated heritage assets, including Lydiard House (listed as Grade I), the Church of St. Mary (listed at Grade I) and the listed garden structures situated within it.'

Bringing the parlous state of Lydiard's financial affairs more up-to-date, 2014 saw rumours rife that Swindon Borough Council was considering selling off Lydiard House and Park in a cost-cutting, out-sourcing exercise. Amidst strenuous denial of these rumours, the local authority soon announced plans to lease out the house and parkland. To most residents this amounted to much the same thing. It seemed as if the council, unlike its predecessor the Swindon Corporation, didn't appreciate the worth of the heritage site.

Her Majesty The Queen at the entrance to Lydiard House in 2005 when she met those involved in the restoration project. (Richard Wintle, Calyx Multimedia)

Following the 2015 Swindon Borough Council shock announcement, the local authority confirmed that they were looking for potential prospective partners to take on the day-to-day running of Lydiard House and Park. The aim being to create more commercial opportunities. The

Sarah Finch-Crisp, former keeper of the house and a key driver of the Lydiard Park restoration project, in the walled garden

response by Swindon residents was immediate. An online petition raised by the Friends of Lydiard Park soon received 10,000 signatures. Then a public meeting attended by more than 700 people, followed hot on its heels.

By 2017 the remit appeared to change and Swindon Borough Council began to favour a community-based not-for-profit trust to take charge. The Lydiard Park Heritage Trust found itself chosen as the preferred bidder. And then in 2018 Swindon Borough Council made a surprise announcement to abandon the outsourcing process and to retain control of the estate.

Is the oft-quoted jewel in the crown of Swindon safe? Despite the promises, total reassurance is difficult.

The Coach House Tea Rooms: Lydiard Park

Frederick, 2nd Viscount Bolingbroke (1732–1787) had expensive tastes. With the family fortunes pretty much intact Frederick set about spending it all. He enjoyed partying, collecting Sevres porcelain and he especially enjoyed gambling and racehorses. Frederick had a stable at Newmarket but enlarged those at Lydiard Park to accommodate his ever-increasing string of racehorses. Estimates put his acquisition of horses, during a five-year period, in the 1760s, at around seventy.

The remaining stable block alongside the walled garden is a 19th-century building. It underwent conversion into the coach house tea rooms during the 2005-7 Lydiard Park Restoration Project. The building also accommodates an education room funded by the BMW group as part of their involvement in the restoration programme.

In 1806, following the death of Charlotte the wife he abandoned, George Richard, 3rd Viscount Bolingbroke (1761–1824) returned to Lydiard House. After an absence of many years George Richard set about making some changes to his country mansion. A year of negotiation between the Viscount and the church authorities saw George Richard receive permission to put some space between Lydiard House and the churchyard at St. Mary's. In an exchange of land George was able to push back the boundary of the churchyard, creating a small, private garden behind a wall.

Since the 15th century parishioners had entered the church through the south porch but George objected to the *hoi polloi* walking so

The St Mary's Church rectory, with caretaker's caravan, shortly before the building was demolished in the early 1980s

close to his property. He closed the porch, redirecting access to the church from the north side of the churchyard and through the west door. As part of this deal George Richard built new pathways and walls around the church. He demolished the old, dilapidated rectory and, in its place, he built a stable block for the use of those worshipping at the church. The building remains today and St Mary's uses it for a variety of activities. At his own expense he built a new rectory on a plot of land near the Hay Lane entrance to Lydiard Park. Sadly, the 1990s building of Sleaford and Cleeves Close saw that building demolished.

Other features to visit in Lydiard Park as you walk around the grounds are the ice house and the plunge pool. The Grade II listed ice house stands in a wooded area between Lydiard House and the Forest Cafe. John 2nd Viscount St. John (1702–1748) built the ice house in about 1743 during the Lydiard House remodelling project.

A must-have 18th-century mod con, an ice house not only preserved food but enabled the creation of fashionable desserts such as ice-cream. The Lydiard House ice house is a top of the range design called the Cup & Dome. Servants cut ice taken from the lake and packed it between layers of straw. That process rendered it capable of lasting for eighteen months.

John's son George Richard, 3rd Viscount Bolingbroke, dogged by ill health, built the plunge pool in about 1820. He recognised, as we do today, the health-giving properties of cold-water bathing. In the 19th century the water level of the lake kept the pool topped up.

6
St Mary's Church

Frances Bevan

If Lydiard House is the jewel of Swindon's crown then it's not unreasonable to argue that St Mary's church, next to the original front entrance to the house, is the crown itself. You could get the idea that this church was the St. John's family personal church – so stuffed is it with monuments to them. But no, it's a regular parish church where peasants and yeoman beholden to the St. John family would come to worship God and observe family members in their specially reserved areas, entered via their own entrance, rather than sharing with commoners.

St Mary's, next to Lydiard House. Before the 18th century remodelling, the church stood in front of the original front entrance. The St John's would have entered St Mary's by a side entrance to pews reserved for family and guests to avoid mixing with commoners.

WEST SWINDON

WHAT THE EYE DOESN'T SEE

St. Mary's has been a place of worship for over a thousand years. Grade I listed, the church has features dating from the 11th-century font to the 13th-century wall-paintings. These colourful illustrations played an important role in educating the largely illiterate congregation in the stories from the gospels. Obliterated during the iconoclasm of the Reformation and the English civil wars, remnants of the wall-paintings have been revealed during the 21st-century conservation project. Visit the church and you'll see that its oldest monument is that of the kneeling figures of Nicholas St. John and his wife Elizabeth Blount. Their son John erected it in 1592.

Today, the canopied memorial stands beneath a window in the south aisle. But that wasn't its original position. In the 1630s Sir John St. John, the 1st Baronet, remodelled the south aisle and moved things around. In the ten years that followed, Sir John commissioned a series of magnificent memorials to the St. John family. He began by commissioning a multi-panel artwork that caused the Archbishop of Canterbury, the Most Rev Justin Welby, to stand and stare in amazement on a visit to St. Mary's in 2014.

Paul Gardner, Chair St Mary's Lydiard Tregoze Conservation Project, describing the St John family polyptych to the Archbishop of Canterbury the Most Rev Justin Welby, and Mrs Caroline Welby, on their visit to Lydiard Park in 2014.
(Richard Wintle, Calyx Multimedia)

With help from Sir John's uncle, Sir Richard St George who happened to be an officer of the College of Arms, the St. John family genealogically is colourfully displayed, beginning with Margaret Beauchamp, wife of Oliver St. John in 1420. The artwork has a separate panel celebrating the St. John Tudor connections and prominently includes the Royal coat of arms referencing Queen Elizabeth I's visit to Lydiard House in 1592. At the centre of the polyptych is the most extraordinary family portrait. There exists a suggestion of it being the work of court painter, William Larkin.

Sir John placed his parents John St. John and Lucy Hungerford central to the portrait. It shows the couple kneeling in prayer upon a sarcophagus. Beneath it lies three coffins to represent their children who died in childhood. To the right of the portrait stand Sir John's six sisters while John and his wife stand on the left.

During its long history the portrait has suffered from overpainting. The effects of this were, for the most part, corrected by conservation during the 1980s. Sadly, the face of Anne Leighton, Sir John's first wife, suffered irreparable damage.

The polyptych, mounted on the north wall of the chancel stands opposite the St. John tomb. Installed in 1634, over ten years before Sir John's 1648 death, and made in London, it's thought that the memorial is the work of celebrated Gloucester sculptor, Samuel Baldwin. When the monument arrived at St. Mary's it proved to be too tall for the space allocated and needed some adaptation.

Sir John lies in the centre of the bedlike monument, flanked by his wives. To his left lies his first wife, Anne Leighton and to his right, his second wife, Margaret Whitmore. The monument depicts Anne holding her thirteenth child. Anne died shortly after the birth but the baby survived into adulthood. Margaret Whitmore holds a book in her hands, evidence of her faith and intellect.

At the head of Sir John and Anne stand sculptures of their five surviving sons, while at their feet are the figures of their three daughters. On the side are depictions of the four children who had previously died. There is a full and informative inscription, though the date of Anne's death is recorded as 1638. That's incorrect – she did in fact die in 1628. More of the inscription here:

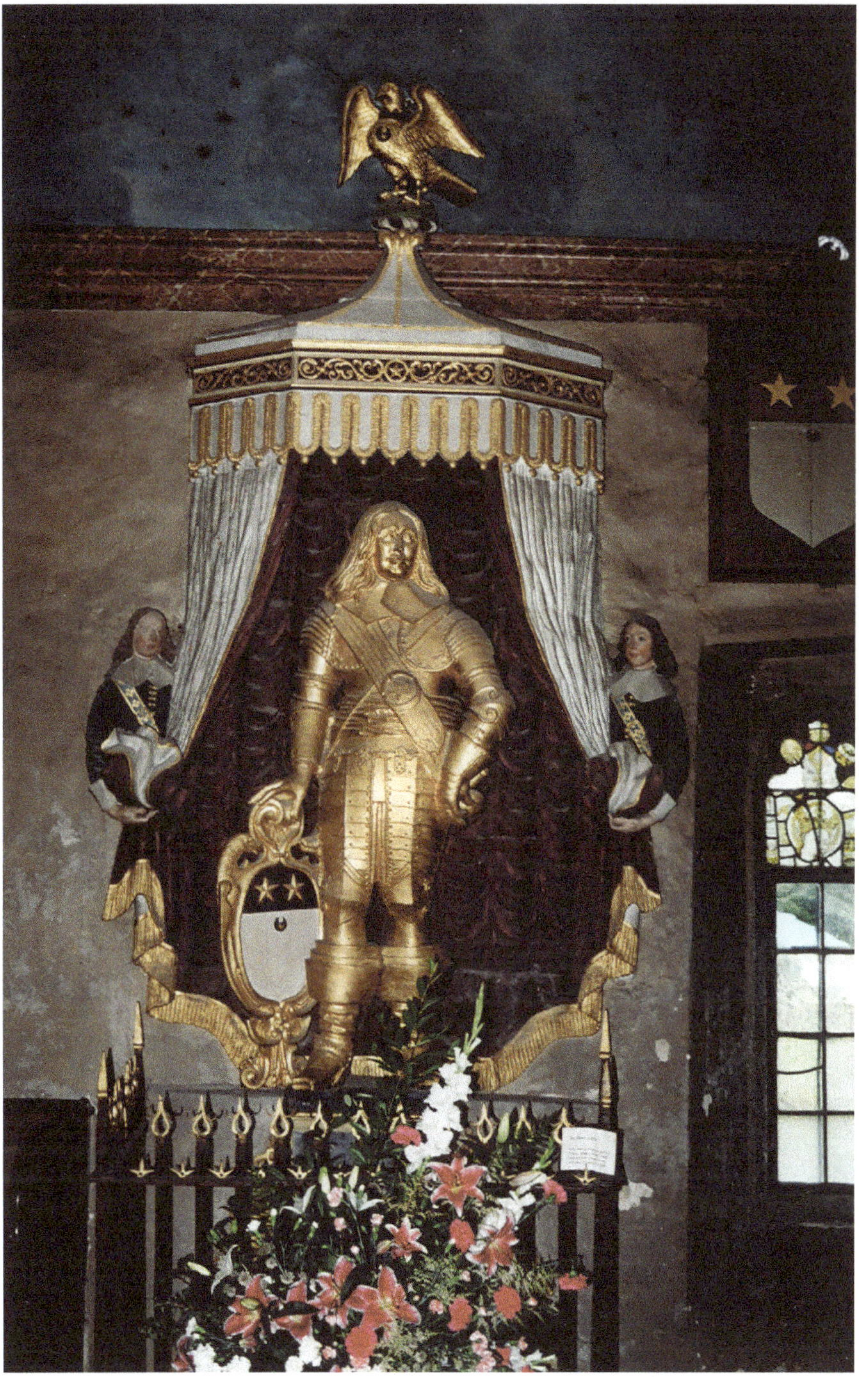

Sacred to God, John St. John, Knight and Baronet, in his 49th year, mindful of his mortal nature, had this marble monument erected in the year 1634, to himself and his two wives, namely Ann and Margaret. Anne was the daughter of Thomas Leighton, Knight, by his wife Elizabeth, of the Knowles family and of the kindred of Queen Elizabeth, as blessed in character as in connection. She lived for thirty-seven years, endowed with noble gifts of mind, body, and manner, a rare example of virtue and piety; she was the mother of thirteen surviving children; in the end, long worn down by the painful agonies of her last confinement and at last overcome, she fled to heaven on 19 September, 1638.

Margaret was the daughter of William Whitmore, Knight, of Apley in the county of Shropshire. In her fifty-eighth year she is still living. Notable for the fame of her virtue and given to good works; she is to be added to the tomb of this family when her time comes - unless she one day otherwise decides.

In 1630 Sir John commissioned the renowned 17th-century glass painter Abraham van Linge to create a window for the east wall of the chancel. He wanted the window made as a monument to his uncle, Oliver St. John, 1st Viscount Grandison. The window includes references to the St. John family name with depictions of John the Baptist and St. John the Divine.

The last of Sir John's magnificent memorials is the one called today the Golden Cavalier. Note though, it wasn't gold when made. That was a Victorian 'improvement.' It's dedicated to Sir John's so-say favourite son, Edward. Like his two elder brothers Edward fought and fell in battle, fighting on the Royalist side in the English Civil Wars. Wounded at the 2nd Battle of Newbury in 1644, he made it home to Lydiard House. There he died, five-and-a-half months later, from his wounds.

While the St. John memorials are the most eye-catching features in the church, there are many other elements to marvel at. Not least of which are the many plaques to other prominent local families. Clear proof that this fascinating building has, at its heart, always been a parish church.

In 2011 St Mary's became the subject of an extensive conservation project. The ten-year project received funding from the National Lottery Heritage Fund with significant support from organisations including

WHAT THE EYE DOESN'T SEE

Painstaking conservation work in St Mary's the Friends of Lydiard Park. Counted among the features conserved we find the medieval wall-paintings, the most significant of which is the Martyrdom of Thomas Becket above the nave.

Sir Simon Jenkins, BBC broadcaster, author and chair of the National Trust 2008-2014, included St. Mary's in his book 'England's Thousand Best Churches,' published in 1999. In it he remarked that 'were the South Chapel removed lock, stock and barrel to the Victoria & Albert Museum in London, it would cause a sensation.

The unusual family portrait and family tree was included by author Simon Jenkins in his book England's Thousand Best Churches

7
The Farms of West Swindon

FRANCES BEVAN

WANDER AROUND West Swindon and remnants of West Swindon's farms will show themselves to you. Toothill Farm and Upper Shaw Farm became community centres, Lower Shaw Farm on Old Shaw Lane is now a cultural and education hub. Though remnants of its previous life, including animals on site, remain. Meanwhile, the Hungry Horse pub restaurant enjoyed a previous existence as Brookhouse Farm.

Farm workers' cottage on Freshbrook Way before renovation as private dwellings

A small number of farm workers' dwellings remain dotted about. They're quite distinctive from everything around them. For instance, on the edge of Lydiard Park and the bottom edge of Grange Park you'll see one – look for the wooden ogee soffits, like the ones on the image here.

Eastleaze and Wick farmhouses are now private dwellings and on Freshbrook Way, once the main road into Swindon, a pair of one-time farm cottages are now family homes.

What follows is the story of those farms and some of the people that lived, loved and died in them.

Boundary changes in the 1970s extended Swindon's western limits into the parish of Lydiard Tregoz – as referred to in old documents. Today we know it as Lydiard Tregoze. The new boundaries included farmland up as far as Lydiard Park and encompassing Shaw and Nine Elms. In less than two decades the area was to alter beyond recognition. Farms such as Toothill and Mannington found themselves swept aside in an ambitious development scheme. This development saw the creation of housing and new village centres adopting ancient farm and field names, transforming an area that had changed little in centuries.

The farms in the Swindon area were predominantly dairy, with arable farming making but a minor contribution to the farmers' income. When Elliot Woolford moved into Hook Farm on the edge of Lydiard Park in 1892, vegetables comprised his primary crop. He also sold fowl and their eggs at Swindon market. Over the years he developed his dairy herd selling his milk to both the Purton Creamery and the Dairy Supply Company in Wootton Bassett. In a farming career that spanned more than fifty years he developed and diversified. Then, as today, farmers adapted to market forces.

The tenant farmers were figures of local authority and each family was serious in its approach to their responsibilities. As parish ratepayers they attended vestry meetings, the local governing body of the day, and served as parish officers. The coming of the railways in the 1840s saw some local men take up employment in the Great Western Railway Works in Swindon. But most continued to work in rural industries and on the farms.

The medieval system of open field strip farming ended with enclosure, the movement to fence in land and create compact, privately-owned holdings. Enclosure in the parish of Lydiard Tregoz took place in the late 16th century. Nicholas St. John instigated it and common fields, commons and marshes of the main manor became enclosed by agreement between local freeholders and tenants. The new system saw increased agricultural production, benefiting the large landowner and tenant farmer but impoverishing the common man.

As living conditions for the poor deteriorated in the large industrial towns and cities, the wealthy during the Georgian and Victorian eras grew ever more nostalgic about the country idyll, reflected in the growth in large estates and the arts and literature of the time. Yet conditions for the rural poor tended to be bleak. They lived in cramped, unhygienic cottages subsisting on inadequate, irregular wages and working long days at hard physical labour.

Early 19th-century vestry records reveal the attempts of the parish to deal with the widespread unemployment. In 1821 the vestry decided to subsidise the wages of those not in regular employment. In 1823, Lord Bolingbroke and Lord Clarendon, major landowners in Lydiard Tregoz, both donated £5 each to buy coal for the poor. The vestry continued to play an important role in overseeing rates of pay in the parish. During the 1820s, rates of pay for mowers during the summer months were agreed in vestry meetings.

In 1825 the vestry ordered that those who employed regular labour must include a certain number of unemployed. Rates of pay were fixed. As late as 1853 the vestry continued sometimes to regulate wages.

Come 1845 the vestry authorised the churchwardens and overseers to raise £8 towards assisting a passage to America for any young man wishing to emigrate. During the following five years, the poor rate also raised money to help those who wished to leave for Australia.

We can trace the history of the parish of Lydiard Tregoz back more than a thousand years. Throughout the history of the two parishes of Lydiard Tregoz and Lydiard Millicent, you can find references to dairy farming and cheese making.

In 1084 the Blackgrove Hundred included Swindon, Wroughton, Lydiard Tregoz and Wootton Bassett. A hundred was the name given to an area of local government and administration in size something between a village and a shire. In about the 16th century Blackgrove, Kingsbridge and Thornhill Hundreds merged under the title Kingsbridge. The name Blackgrove or Blagrove has been around a long time. It survives today in the naming of an industrial estate on the edge of West Swindon, a mere stone's throw from the M4 motorway.

WHAT THE EYE DOESN'T SEE

West Swindon Field Names 1839 - 1843

The drawing shows the field names and boundaries for Toothill, Freshbrook, Grange Park and Westlea. The layout of the new roads and roundabouts built since Swindon's expansion to the west have been added.

Some reference points: Turnpike Road is the old A420 which ran from London to Bristol through Swindon. The modern Tewkesbury Way was built alongside it and Freshbrook Way was built on the original line. Freshbrook Church and Windmill Hill School now block where it emerged next to the present Volvo showroom. The thick lines are various streams running through the area and the railway line can be traced at the bottom of the illustration.
1. Toothill Village Centre; 2. Oliver Tomkins Primary School; 3. Freshbrook School; 4. Westlea School

    Tithes were a payment of one-tenth of the land's produce and it's here that the complications arose. How did a dairy farmer in North Wiltshire pay his tithes – was it a tenth of the milk, butter and cheese he produced or every tenth cow in his herd? The 1956 Collins *New English Dictionary*, states that a tithe pig is one pig in ten, paid as tithe. Hence the smallest pig in a litter is still, with a touch of jest, referred to as the parson's pig.

Tithes were difficult to administer, becoming ever more unpopular to both farmers and rural landowners. By the 19th century they didn't reflect the changing social and economic conditions of the developing industrial era.

In 1836 an act of parliament called the *Tithe Commutation Act* converted tithes into an annual rent on the land linked to the price of cereals, thereby allowing for fluctuations in inflation.

Throughout the 1980s Swindon continued to develop westward towards the M4 encroaching on the neighbouring parish of Wroughton.

Blagrove Farm

The Wroughton estate of Elcombe, with the four Blagrove farms, fell under the ownership of the Compton family. There they remained, until William Compton, 1st Earl of Northampton (1568–1630) peer and politician sold various properties to Thomas Sutton. Sutton founded the Hospital of King James and a school to educate forty boys, which later became known as the Charterhouse School. Included in this sale were Compton's other properties: Whitehill, Mannington and Toothill Farms in the parish of Lydiard Tregoz.

Somewhat confusingly, there appears to have been more than one farmstead in this area, pre-20th century. Thus, West Blagrove was the long-time home of the King family. Francis Tuckey entered the world in Lydiard Millicent in 1738. There the parish registers record 'Francis ye base born son of Briget [sic] Tuckey' baptised at All Saints on 'August ye 8 1738.' Bridget married Francis King when their son was six years old and throughout his life Francis junior went under both surnames. Sometimes he signed himself Francis King, sometimes Tuckey. And sometimes Francis King *alias* Tuckey. The Tuckey family was a wealthy, local, landowning family so it's possible Francis just wanted to keep his options open.

It would appear that Francis King, otherwise Tuckey, married three times. His first wife was Elizabeth Dore whom he married by licence on 29 May 1769 at St Mary's Church, Lydiard Tregoz. Elizabeth was the mother of Richard Dore King who bears her maiden name. Wife number two was Jane Cole. An entry in St Mary's parish registers lists

WHAT THE EYE DOESN'T SEE

Francis King married Jane Cole by licence on 21 October 1773. Francis married for a third time, again by licence at St Mary's, to Ann Hedges on 24 November 1784. These dates would tally with the birth of three of the children mentioned in his will. Ann born in 1785, John in 1787 and Mary in 1789.

Francis died on 2 March 1808 at the farm at Blagrove. He was 69 years old. In 1871 the farm remained in the occupancy of the King family. There Francis's granddaughter Sarah Sheppard King farmed 340 acres and employed six men and three boys.

Marsh Farm

In the 19th century a near neighbour of Blagrove Farm was Marsh Farm, part of the Lydiard Estate owned by Viscount Bolingbroke. In 1841 the farm comprised a little over 115 acres of land. They had two fields named The Shannells and Far Shannells and others with more prosaic names such as The Ten Acres and the Eight Acres - for obvious reasons.

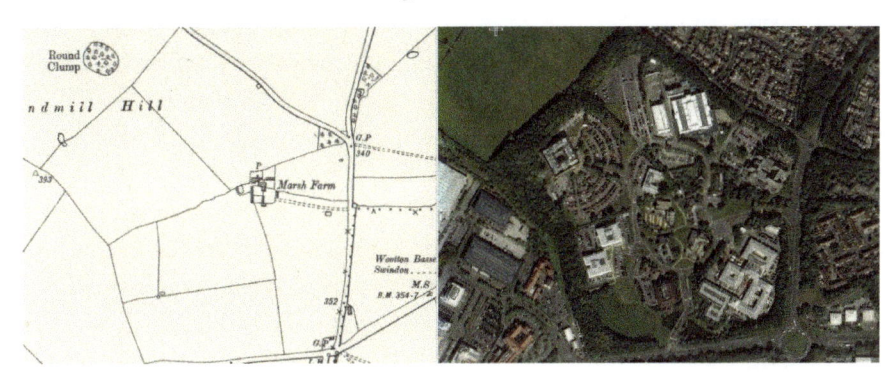

Marsh Farm then & now. On the left, set within farm fields. On the right, at the centre of Windmill Hill Business Park off Whitehill Way (National Library of Scotland).

The dairy farming area of Lydiard Millicent and Lydiard Tregoz contained a small, close-knit community. For most families their working and social lives centred on the local parish church. Farming families worked long hours and had little time for socialising. When they did take time to relax it was with family members, friends and neighbours.

Families had intermarried down the generations and bonds of kinship were strong. Prosperous, landowning families would think with care about who their children married – they wanted their investments to be well looked after. Parents would advise their sons and daughters on who would make a good match – who would most likely prove to be a good husband or wife. Daughters in particular carried the burden of expectation of following their father's wishes.

Of great help to researchers, the maiden name of the wife was often included in the naming of their children. Often a woman was already pregnant at the time of her marriage, with the baby's birth registered less than nine months after the couple's wedding. Farmers and landowners were keen to know that their wife, like their land, was fertile.

The tenant at Marsh Farm in 1841 was James Ellison. But by 1851 he had moved to Lower Studley Farm and Marsh was under the tenure of Abraham Humphries. In 1842 Abraham Humphries married Elizabeth Bathe King, the daughter of his neighbours at Blagrove, Richard and Elizabeth King. Abraham died in May 1858 at the age of 43 and he's buried in St. Mary's churchyard in a grave marked by a Grade II listed chest tomb monument.

Elizabeth retained her interest in Marsh Farm but her second marriage to Jonas Clarke Jnr from Wick Farm proved unsuccessful. Jonas embarked upon an affair with his cousin Kate, and at length moved away from the area. Elizabeth remained at Marsh Farm until sometime in the 1860s and by 1871 Francis Carey (a relative of the Clarke family) farmed 113 acres. Records show a succession of short-term tenancies at Marsh Farm, until the arrival of William J. Rumming at the end of the 19th century. His son John succeeded him at Marsh Farm and would buy the property when Lady Bolingbroke sold large tracts of the Lydiard Estate in 1930.

The Windmill Hill Business Park now stands on the site of Marsh Farm, although the farmhouse still remains. But the windmill is not an original feature; it came from Chiseldon in 1984. *See the buildings section for more about the windmill.*

Toothill Farm

The development of West Swindon began with the former Charterhouse lands. 'A 300-acre site at Toot Hill south of the A420 Swindon to Wootton Bassett road will provide the homes in a new urban village,' the *Swindon Advertiser* reported on Wednesday 17 November 1971 as Thamesdown Council received approval for the western expansion of the town.

The milking parlour at Toothill Farm before demolition, similar to such buildings at farms across the western expansion

Toothill is an Old English name for a meeting place, look-out point or watchtower, and is referred to the Bible. In the first edition of the *Link* magazine published in December 1978, (published initially as the *Toothill Link* newsletter), church worker Olive King explained that the word appears several times in the late 14th-century Wycliffe Bible, the first translation into English. For instance, Isaiah 21, verse 5 states, 'Sett the bord, behold in a toothill or 'Prepare the table, watch in a watchtower.'

We see the first mention of a farm on this site in 1594. Antiquarian John Aubrey (1627-97) identified Toothill as the site of the ancient Antiock's Well, famous for its miraculous and healing properties.

Toothill Farm has had many owners and occupiers during its long history. It's a fact of some remark that letters concerning the 18th-century tenancy dispute have survived. In a box of Charterhouse documents held at the London Metropolitan Archives in Clerkenwell, an exchange of letters between Jasper Yorke, David Smith and Thomas Melmouth records the contested lease of the farm at Toothill. At the time of the 19th-century *Tithe Commutation Act*, recorded field names include Withy Bed, Little Toot Hill, The Hospital and Last Field. While several fields were simply called 'New Inclosure' indicating the reorganisation of land.

Toothill Farm, c1975, during construction of the Great Western Way, before the sound barrier was built

In 1919 Wiltshire County Council bought Toothill Farm along with the other Charterhouse properties. The authority converted them into smallholdings for soldiers returning from service in the First World War.

In advance of new housebuilding, archaeological excavations in 1974/5 found evidence of a small medieval village to the east of Toothill farm. House platforms, a stone-lined well, stone footings and a hollow

Toothill Farm: the cart shed, now demolished, and the livestock barn, now used as a Scout hut

way (a medieval thoroughfare) were among the features later destroyed during development.

The view from the farmhouse once took in the land to the south of the town all the way to Wroughton. Farmworkers would have witnessed the digging of the canal, the laying of the railway line and the construction of the Great Western Way. Today the farmhouse and its surrounding field, a Swindon Borough Council owned property, sits tucked away next to Bodiam Drive. In 1979 the derelict cart shed and milking parlour were demolished, though the barn managed to survive and underwent conversion into first a youth club and later a meeting place for cubs and scouts.

Mannington Farm
In 1835 Richard Strange signed a twelve-year lease on the 237-acre Mannington Farm. There he would remain as tenant farmer for more than forty-five years. Following his death in 1883 his daughter Julia took over for a further ten years. The Strange family have a long history in Swindon, playing a prominent role in both commerce and nonconformity in the town. James Strange was the founder of the Newport Street Independent Chapel built in 1804. The family were salt and coal merchants, grocers and drapers. They even opened the first bank in Swindon in 1807 called Strange, Garrett, Strange and Cook.

Agricultural labourer, James Pitt was first employed by tenant farmer Richard Dore King at Mannington Farm. His wife Elizabeth and five daughters soon joined the payroll, working in a variety of roles as housemaid, cook and lady's maid. Following Jane Pitt's marriage to coachman Thomas Osman their two daughters Louisa and Julia were also employed in the farmhouse. The Pitt and Osman families notched up an incredible combined service of over 160 years extending across three generations.

Jane Osman died in April 1899, buried in Radnor Street cemetery, her sister Martha Pitt and her husband Thomas Osman both joined her there in 1909. Their grave is one plot removed from the Strange family grave, neighbours in death as they were in life.

Today the elegant 18th-century farmhouse that the Pitt girls cleaned and polished is flats and a bus lane passes by where the family cottage once stood.

Whitehill Farm

Records for Whitehill Farm date back to the 17th century when John Lawe farmed 65 acres in 1616. In 1799 Richard Dore King signed a twelve-year Lady Day lease on the farm. There the wealthy King family remained in residence for much of the 19th century along with their other farm at Blagrove. Like Mannington and Toothill Farm, Whitehill found itself converted into small holdings for soldiers returning from the First World War battlefields. Wilfred Parsons became the first post-war tenant at Whitehill when he returned from service in Egypt.

During the Second World War Whitehill Farm was home to an army camp with soldiers billeted on one of the fields and later both German and Italian prisoners of war. The facilities were basic, with no NAAFI for the soldiers. Farmer's wife Mrs Parsons provided them with provisions while the officers used the farm parlour as a living room. Three anti-aircraft guns and a machine gun once sat in the field that's now Kiln Park.

Brook Farm

It's fortunate that some of the farmhouses escaped demolition and survive today as private homes, community centres and pubs. One such building is Brook House Farm. Throughout its history Brook Farm, as it was until the beginning of the 20th century, has perched on the boundary of the two Lydiard parishes. A farmhouse on the present site dates back to at least the 18th century, making an appearance on the 1773 Andrews and Dury map of Wiltshire where it's named simply The Brook. The pasture land belonging to Brook Farm is also indicated on the Lydiard Estate Map of 1773.

The 1841 tithe map for Lydiard Millicent details over 119 acres of land belonging to John Lewis Mallet. These fields of pasture bore such colourful names as Great Shelfinch, Tumpy, The Mead, Middle Leaze and Ram Leaze. These names became adopted as place names in the 1980s development. Here also are two cottages with gardens, an orchard and, standing in over one acre of land, is the homestead and its garden. The tenant of the farm was Thomas Plummer. The tithe map for Lydiard Tregoz details a further fifty acres of pasture owned by Lord Bolingbroke and farmed by Thomas Plummer.

Brook Farmhouse, before redevelopment as a restaurant

Brook Farm was again auctioned at the Goddard Arms Hotel, Swindon, in 1901 when the owner was Joses Badcock. The auction listing describes the farm as a 'high class residential pasture farm . . . comprising Picturesque House with Gardens and grounds, Farm Buildings, Cottages, and Pasture Lands having a total area of about 165a 2r 33p.'

On the ground floor there's a drawing room, a dining room and a morning room as well as a large entrance hall. On the first floor there are five bedrooms and a large box room. On the second floor (the attic) there are two servants' bedrooms.

Brook Farm had a handful of owners during the first half of the 20th century, among them Miss Elizabeth Akers, Alfred Leonard Purkis and Harold Pears.

Today Brook House Farm stands on the corner of Middleleaze Drive, one of the former field names adopted for the new housing development. With views across Lydiard Park and with its back to the sprawling town of Swindon, Brook House Farm straddles the divide between town and country.

Wick Farm

It's arguable that the earliest reference to a farmstead in the Wick Farm area was in 1235 when Robert Tregoz owned the manor. Although it's possible that the present site has associations going back much further as *wic* is a Saxon word meaning dairy. During the 14th century the de Wyk family leased the farm.

Wick Farm also appears on the Andrews and Dury map with the present farmhouse described as having elements dating from the 16th century.

The Victorian tenant most associated with Wick Farm is Jonas Clarke whose grave is just inside the churchyard gate at St. Mary's. Jonas Clarke was born in Oaksey where he married Elizabeth Fitchew, a widow, on 14 November 1816. But by the time he arrived at Wick Farm he was living with Anne Pinnell. With divorce unavailable to most, when a marriage broke down the only option for a couple who could not wed was to live together. Jonas Clarke had to wait for his first wife Elizabeth to die before he could marry Alice Pinnell, the woman he'd lived with for over thirty years and the mother of his seven children.

Deposited at the Wiltshire and Swindon History Centre in

WHAT THE EYE DOESN'T SEE

Wick Farm with livestock, with housing at Middleleaze and Shaw in the background

Chippenham are two pocket sized notebooks which contain the rough farm accounts for Wick Farm. One dates from the 1840s and 50s and one from the 1860s. Among the entries are the names of dairy cattle 'bulled' from February to June 1846 and the number of cheeses stored in the cheese room above the dairy.

In 1930 Lady Bolingbroke sold a large part of the Lydiard Park estate. These are the details for Lot 28 Wick Farm taken from the sale catalogue:

> An exceedingly dry rich grazing and dairy holding known as WICK FARM situate in the Parishes of Lydiard Tregoz and Lydiard Millicent, and having an acreage of 139a 1r 3p intersected by good roads.
>
> The Farm House is brick built, slated and tiled and the farm buildings are of similar construction. There are also two excellent modern cottages substantial built of brick, with slated roofs, each containing five rooms. This farm has been in hand recently and, for the purposes of this sale, the rent is estimated at £332. Vacant possession can be given on completion.

On 25 March 1963, Douglas Perrin Story bought Wick Farm. He held the property in trust for the Building and Public Works Construction Company.

Peter Cove was the last tenant when, in 1971, Swindon Borough Council bought it and Upper Shaw Farm, for £156,080. At the time of the sale Wick Farm consisted of four fields and was the last working dairy farm in West Swindon.

In 1988/89, ahead of the planned West Swindon development, an archaeological investigation began on the surrounding area. Wick farmhouse became the base for the Thamesdown Archaeological Unit. Evidence of the Romano-British pottery industry was discovered in a neighbouring field named Blacklands. The removal of clay for pottery would account for the large number of ponds on the 20th-century farm. More Romano-British features revealed themselves in a field called High Croft during the construction of the new road.

Plans were submitted in 1985 and 1992 to use the farmhouse as a Christian Centre but the local authority rejected them. At length the property fell into private hands.

Field names such as High Croft and the Clay Pit Ground have disappeared beneath the 1980s development. But local housing estates, such as *The Prinnells* and *Bakers Mead*, adopted others.

Shaw Farm

Shaw Farm was one of three farms clustered together where the two parishes of Lydiard Millicent and Lydiard Tregoz converged.

An indenture dated 23 June 1809 between Robert Hughes and Thomas Packer Butt of Arle Court, Gloucestershire provides useful information when tracing the history of this farm, once called Bailey's Farm and occupied by Christopher Strange. See chapter 3 on open spaces and public art, for more on what became of this site.

Roughmoor Farm

The Peatmoor area in which Roughmoor Farm once sat was a later development in the West Swindon expansion and didn't get started until the late 1980s.

The history of Roughmoor Farm (sometimes called Row Moor) dates back to at least 1596 when Anthony Ashley owned it. Roughmoor was never a very large farm, measuring between 86 acres in the mid-19th century to a little over 72 acres in 1974. The farm stood at the edge of Peatmoor Copse. Today there stands there a small fragment of the

WHAT THE EYE DOESN'T SEE

ancient Royal Bradon Forest that once extended across North Wiltshire.

At the beginning of the 19th century Roughmoor, Sparcells and Lower Shaw Farms belonged to the Shaftesbury family. Stephen Cole and his wife Sarah were tenant farmers at Roughmoor from at least the time of their marriage in 1804. Following Stephen's death in 1822 Sarah continued running the farm with her son John.

In 1825 Cropley Ashley-Cooper, 6th Earl of Shaftesbury, sold the three farms to Sir Robert Buxton. Sir Robert's grandson (another Sir Robert) disposed of them in a series of sales some forty years later. He sold Sparcells in 1864. Roughmoor went in portions from 1865-70 and Lower Shaw Farm went under the hammer sometime around 1870.

The new owner and occupier at Roughmoor was James Hughes, Stephen and Sarah Cole's grandson. Following James's death his

Roughmoor Farm in the late 1980s. The farmhouse, off Swinley Drive, was demolished in the early 2000s to make way for new housing

mortgagees sold the farm to Mary Haines, his wife Catherine's sister-in-law. The farm remained in the extended family. Hence, when Mary died in 1918 it passed to her daughter Mary Gladys Haines. That same year Mary Gladys Haines sold it to Stephen Edward Cole, another of Stephen and Sarah's grandsons. When Stephen Edward Cole died in 1936 the farm had been in the occupancy of one family for more than 130 years.

In 1957 Roughmoor Farm, comprising 72.5 acres, was conveyed to Mr John Hedley Jones. In 1973 he sold it to a company called Superior Developments Ltd. A year later, Swindon Borough Council, for the sum of £1.4 million, acquired Roughmoor, Lower Shaw Farm and Sparcells farm, totalling 286 acres approximately. They did that under the Town Development Act, 1952.

Roughmoor Farm was one of seven farms in the parish of Lydiard Millicent transferred to Swindon Borough Council in the 1980s for the purpose of development – a total of 759 acres.

In the early 1970s the Breakthrough Trust (Deaf-Hearing Integration) charity occupied the farmhouse. Run by Libbie Sheppard and centre director Terry Waters, the Trust ran a programme of day and weekend events. It closed in 1989 and the farmhouse was later demolished. A cul-de-sac of executive homes built on the site retains the name Roughmoor Farm Close.

Sparcells Farm

Sparcells Farm lends its name to an area that once marked the boundary of Lydiard Millicent and Purton. In the mid 19th century Sparcells Farm measured 118 acres. The farmhouse and 42 acres stood in the parish of Purton. Meanwhile farm buildings and a further 76 acres were in Lydiard Millicent.

Following the 1864 sale, Corsham farmer Walter Edwards bought Sparcells. When Walter died in 1893 he left the farm to his two sons, the elder of whom, also named Walter, took over the day to day running.

Lower Shaw Farm

One of four farms located in the hamlet of Shaw along what was once the main road to the village of Lydiard Millicent, Lower Shaw Farm and several other properties in Lydiard Millicent and Purton, formed part of the estate belonging to the Earl of Shaftesbury. One of the early

Lower Shaw Farm with modern day residents at the front door

references to Shaw Farm, as it was then called, is in the will of Thomas Strange, proved in 1710/11. In it he leaves the tenancy of the farm to his niece Bridget Tuckey née Strange and her brother Richard to 'share and share alike.'

Lower Shaw farmhouse is a Grade II listed building. In 1989 a survey of the property dated the house to the mid 18th century. When Robert Tuckey signed the 1789 lease, it's likely this is the house he would have lived in.

The house is on two floors with large attic rooms in the roof. Inside there remains old board and panelled doors and there are some old floor boards on the first floor and in the attic. The brickwork of the original building is described as Flemish bond. That's where bricks lay in an alternating pattern of headers and stretchers creating a checkerboard effect.

The half-hipped roof has corniced brick ridge stacks to outer rear wings and the chimney on the right has a diamond shaped stone engraved 1787, probably the date of former repairs.

During the subsequent 300 years the farmhouse underwent extension and alteration. The late 18th early 19th centuries saw the addition of a cheese room to the rear of the house. The farm outbuildings date from the 20th century. They're built against a former yard wall, that, at the 1989 time of the writing of the report, included a former bread oven.

Following the acquisition of Lower Shaw Farm by the local authority in the 1970s, the farmhouse, outbuildings and three acres of land were leased to the Foundation for Alternatives in Urban Development. That organisation emphasised the importance of adopting a sustainable lifestyle. In 1980 the running of the centre transferred to a local group led by Matt Holland and Andrea Hirsch. For more than forty years, Lower Shaw Farm has been a cultural and education centre for weekend breaks, events and courses, and for thirty years until 2022 it was home to the prestigious Swindon Festival of Literature.

The rear of the farmhouse and repurposed outbuildings around the farmyard

In the front garden there stands a magnificent yew tree. Yew trees are slow growing, and it's believed that this one is somewhere in the region of 300 years old. This would put it in the era of the first Tuckey tenants at the beginning of the 18th century.

In 2005 Swindon Borough Council considered ending the lease and selling the site for development. The proposal was met by major protests from the community and supporters from across the country. The council reconsidered the idea and agreed a long-term lease to allow the farm to continue in its present use.

Upper Shaw Farm before redevelopment in the late 1970s.

Upper Shaw Farm

One of the earliest surviving documents referring to Upper Shaw Farm is the 1841 Tithe Map and Apportionment for Lydiard Millicent. The property was then owned by the Trustees of the late Thomas Packer Butt and comprised 90 acres. The tenant Thomas Sadler farmed at Upper Shaw Farm for 43 years, until his death in 1852. Then, in 1870 William Plummer bought the 74-acre Upper Shaw Farm. William Plummer and his two unmarried sisters grew up at neighbouring Eastleaze Farm where William continued to work both farms. In the Receiving Rentals records of the Bolingbroke estate, W. Plummer still paid £500 annual rent on East Leaze Farm up to and including 1876.

On 24 October 1898 the firm of T. Lavington, Auctioneer, Valuer and Estate Agent with offices at Marlborough and Devizes, made an inventory and valuation of Upper Shaw Farm. The tenancy was changing hands and the new tenant was Mr Allen Hart.

Upper Shaw Farm changed hands several times during the middle of the 20th century with different farmers leaving their mark. The Rebbeck family were owners and occupiers during the 1930s and left their name on a spot on the local landscape once known as Rebbeck's Hill. In 1960 Robert Henry Hook and his brother Walter Charles sold the farm to Charles John Winstone and his son Eric for £11,200. In 1963 the farm went to The Building & Public Works Construction Co., who became the landlords and the Winstone's, once the owners, now became the tenants.

In February 1971 the Mayor, Alderman & Burgesses of the Borough of Swindon bought Upper Shaw Farm along with Wick Farm. The two farms comprised an area of 155.8 acres lying to the west of the Borough boundary within the villages of Shaw and Lydiard Tregoz. The purpose of acquisition was town development.

The farmhouse with modern extension in the late 1980s

Today the former Upper Shaw farmhouse, opposite Shaw Ridge Primary School, survives as a community facility, with a modern hall attached to the original building. It acted as a community centre for

Westlea and Shaw and later as a short breaks respite centre supporting families with children and young people with special educational needs and disabilities.

East Leaze Farm

In the 19th century the three farms in Shaw were somewhat confusingly all referred to as Shaw Farm in contemporary documents. All three straddled the parish boundary of Lydiard Tregoz and Lydiard Millicent, with Lower Shaw Farm and Upper Shaw Farm in Lydiard Millicent and East Leaze Farm in Lydiard Tregoz.

The death of Henry St. John, 4th Viscount Bolingbroke, in 1851 saw the drawing up of an Abstract of Title. This document provides a detailed account of the Lydiard estate dating back to 1789 when both East Leaze and Shaw Farm (alias Bailey's Farm) were owned by the St. John family.

The Victorian census returns reveal that the Sadler and Plummer families occupied both East Leaze and Upper Shaw Farms. In 1804 Richard Plummer married Mary Sadler and their descendants would see a joining of many of several local farming families. Richard and Mary farmed at Shaw and throughout the 19th century the Sadler, Plummer and Cole families were tenants at East Leaze, Shaw and Upper Shaw Farms. In the Receiving Rentals records of the Bolingbroke estate, W. Plummer still paid £500 annual rent on East Leaze Farm up to and including 1876. In 1879 John Clark is recorded as the tenant at 'East Leaze – late Plummer.'

By 1891 William Alfred Rebbeck, a farmer from the village of Overton near Marlborough, was at East Leaze where his son William Henry Enion remained for more than 35 years.

The 1930 Lydiard Estate sale took place at the Goddard Arms Hotel on Friday 21 March. In that sale, Lady Bolingbroke sold off more than 1,800 acres including nine dairy farms in what was described as 'one of the largest sales held in Swindon for many years.' The sale particulars described East Leaze with two cottages, measuring 197 acres with a brick built and slated farmhouse containing hall, three rooms, kitchen, dairy, pantry, back kitchen, mess room cellar, store room and five bedrooms with a large attic. There was tie up accommodation for fifty-six cows, calving boxes, open stalls and yards. Stabling for eight horses and a range of four pigstys. Yet, no offer came for East Leaze Farm, Shaw let to Mr. W.A. Rebbeck, according to the report published in the *North Wilts Herald*, Friday 28 March 1930.

Today East Leaze farmhouse is a private property in Stonefield Close just opposite a branch of the Aldi supermarket chain.

Old Shaw Lane

In this section about West Swindon's farms on the Lydiard Estate, you read about Lower Shaw Farm and Upper Shaw farm. It'll surprise you not at all to learn that they lie on Old Shaw Lane. This little slice of yesteryear buffering modern West Swindon warrants some mention.

The history of Shaw dates back to Domesday. In the middle ages it consisted of around twelve farmsteads that stood along a lane. By 1668 residents knew this lane as Shaw Street.

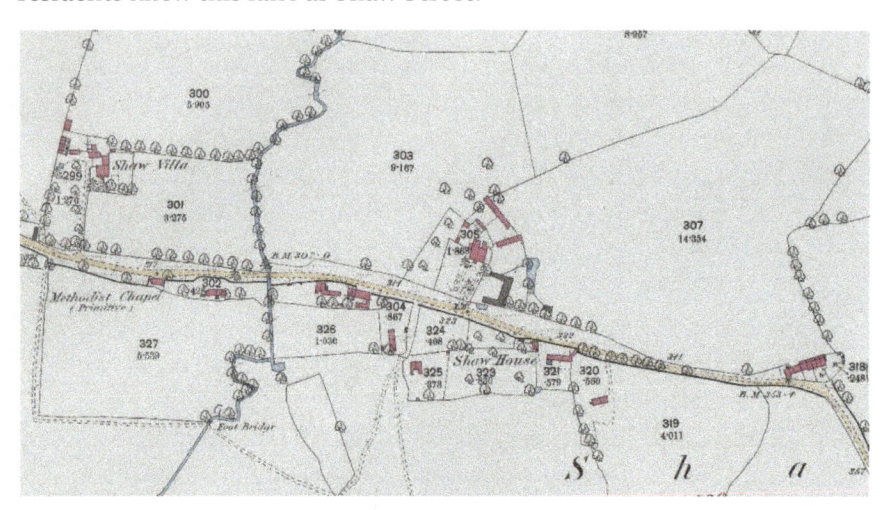

The 1899 Ordnance Survey map illustrating fields and properties around Old Shaw Lane

The two oldest properties on Old Shaw Lane are Lower Shaw Farmhouse and Shaw House. They stand opposite one another, both at one time associated with the Tuckey family.

Thomas Tuckey inherited Shaw House from his father Richard. At that time the property was described as 'Messuage or tenement Garden and Orchard situate and being in Shaw in the Parish of Liddiard Millicent.'

Thomas's mother Johanna lived here during her widowhood, then his sister Mary spent the last years of her life here. Shaw House would remain in the Tuckey family occupation until the death of Ann Tuckey in 1886. By 1891 Shaw House had become the village Club House occupied by William Hollick who still lived there in 1901 when it had the description of a Workman's Club.

The Primitive Methodist chapel on Old Shaw Lane which opened in 1852. It closed in the 1980s when Holy Trinity Church at Shaw Village Centre was built. The chapel was then used by community activities before conversion to a private dwelling in the early 2000s

Building projects during the 19th century saw the addition of Hinton Cottages, Colliers Row and a Primitive Methodist Chapel in Nine Elms. At the end of the century Henry Carter bought parcels of land on which he built a bakery and later the Nine Elms pub. See chapter 8 on buildings for more on that.

After World War II most of the local farms continued to operate, and Shaw and Nine Elms remained small villages on the outskirts of Swindon. Despite rapid development in the nearby town, a journey to

Lydiard Millicent still provided a Sunday afternoon trip into the country for many families. But change was in the air.

In 1966 Wiltshire County Planning Department conducted a survey of rural settlements in the Swindon countryside. The area of Shaw and Washpool became included in the larger parish of Lydiard Millicent. In 1966 the population of these two small settlements was a mere 250. Shaw and Washpool had one general store, a pub and a doctor's surgery. There was a daily bus service and the village was on mains water and electricity but without mains gas. In 1966 the council had recently granted planning permission for two dwellings. Those two houses would increase the population by approximately six people.

As the second phase of the expansion focused on Shaw, in the early 1980s borough council planners proposed a footbridge to link the two parts of Old Shaw Lane which was to be bisected by Roughmoor Way. The idea didn't proceed beyond a model of the scheme after residents objected on the grounds that it was too modern.

The character of Shaw and Washpool had the description of 'scattered communities owing their existence to the pressure of Swindon' – an opinion that ignored the history of the area and was quite inaccurate. As to the future, the council foresaw 'no expansion in present form'. Although they added the area was 'likely to be included in the Swindon expansion, to which there would be no objection.'

And, sure enough, boundary changes in the 1970s extended the Swindon western limits to include the surrounding farmland up as far

Instead of a bridge the two sections of Old Shaw Lane were joined by a pedestrian controlled light

as Lydiard Park and included the villages of Shaw and Nine Elms. But everything was soon to change.

The western development nibbled away at the surrounding fields right up to the back gardens of the cottages, yet Old Shaw Lane continues to preserve an old country appearance. As the re-routed Shaw Road bypassed the old one along Cartwright Drive, the thoroughfare became known as Old Shaw Lane. To this day it retains some country settlement charm.

8
The Twentieth Century Buildings

Angela Atkinson

To bring this West Swindon story up to date, we leap into the 20th century to take a look at sixteen of the area's interesting buildings in a chronological list. That said, the sharp-eyed amongst you will notice that the first one predates the eponymous 100-year period somewhat. But, not fitting anywhere else in this volume, here it is.

The Windmill on Windmill Hill Business Park – 1820s

If one didn't know any better, it would be reasonable to suppose, given its name, that the Windmill Hill business park (a stone's throw from the M4) is so called because there stands a windmill on the site. It further would be reasonable to suppose that the windmill in question had stood there since time immemorial. And indeed, reflected in, and hiding amongst, the shiny, glass-fronted office buildings, the windmill gives every impression of having stood there for decades in solitary splendour until the business park grew up around it. But it deceives. So, while you'd be right in your first assumption you'd be wrong in the second. Because the windmill in question began life in the fields of Chiseldon, around six miles from where it stands now.

Indeed, if you're hoping to find anything on the business park site that ever was there, you'll find it in the form of the Marsh farmhouse now deployed as office accommodation. It and the titular windmill nestle among the futuristic buildings of the business park, serving as wonderful reminders of the past. See chapter 7 on West Swindon's farms for more about this building and its inhabitants.

Built in the 1820s and sited adjacent to Chiseldon's Butts Road

Chiseldon Windmill in the late 19th Century

cemetery, the windmill passed out of use somewhere around 1892 and henceforth became pressed into service as a stable and storage facility.

A ballpark figure for the total cost of constructing the mill in the early 1820s would have looked like £450-500. That would have included the tower, windows, doors, floors, gearing and grinding stones. Such a sum would also have included a set of easy-to-operate shutter sails and even white limewash for the interior walls.

But why did the windmill get relocated to the business park? To answer that question, we need to return to the early 1980s. Back then, there existed a plan for a gleaming new business park for the 80-acre Marsh Farm, in the parish of Lydiard Tregoz. The company behind the £100 million scheme, Kuwaiti-owned St Martin's Property Corporation, had already hit upon a catchy name for its showpiece development – Windmill Hill. The one-time existence of a medieval post mill on the site provided the rationale. Thus, that traditional business activity gave the name to the centre and the reason to move the Chiseldon windmill to where it stands now. After all, what better to contrast with all the modernity than an actual, genuine windmill?

The developers acquired the windmill in 1983 for £15,000. And the fine folk of Chiseldon – who gained funding for tennis courts as part of

The newly rebuilt windmill reflected in the glass offices at the business park

the deal – waved farewell to their 160-year-old landmark. Its thousands of bricks needed careful numbering to make sure each one went back in the right place. Had that not happened it wouldn't have been the Chiseldon windmill but simply an old windmill.

With re-pointed, cleaned-up bricks, spanking new sails, a concrete base, smart door and windows and even a fan tail, it arose from the dead at its new West Swindon home the following year. The process of relocating the windmill wasn't all plain sailing – as it were. Severe damp broke out necessitating drastic action with a special type of mortar.

The five-year rescue-and-restore mission wound-up in 1988, signalling the completion of Swindon's first newly erected windmill.

The Nine Elms Pub – c.1900

The Nine Elms pub at the west end of Old Shaw Lane serves up not only pints and pork scratchings but a reminder of times before the railway came. It's located close to the junction where, in 1766, a lane from Shaw Street joined the Cricklade to Marlborough Road.

Frances Bevan, for the *Swindon Advertiser,* wrote:

> At the end of the 19th century, former Brook Farm farm bailiff William Breadmore sold land at Nine Elms to Henry Carter. Carter built various properties in the hamlet, including a bakery where he later set up business, and the Nine Elms public house.
>
> A visit to the Nine Elms pub once constituted a walk at leisure into the Wiltshire countryside for those living in nearby Swindon, providing the landlord with a thriving passing trade.
>
> By 1915 Tom Boulton and his wife Ellen were the licensees. Villagers remembered the couple as a miserable pair but they may have had good cause. Tom and Ellen's eldest son, Herbert, a private in the Shropshire Light Infantry, had been killed in action during the First World War.

Frances also points out that there's nothing to confirm any notion of the hamlet having taken its name from a group of elm trees at the road junction. They were felled after a 1928 storm brought one of them down, killing a Mr and Mrs Ponting, the occupants of a car trapped underneath it.

Despite the closure of Old Shaw Lane as a through road with the 1980s housing development, thereby reducing the amount of passing traffic, the Nine Elms pub survives and thrives.

Windmill Hill Business Park – 1980s

Little more than a stone's throw from the M4's Junction 16, lies the 80-acre Windmill Hill business park. The site's website describes it as an imaginative collection of high-quality office buildings set in a landscaped business park setting. This collection of futuristic business buildings have watching over them an old windmill, dismantled brick-by-numbered-brick from nearby Chiseldon and rebuilt with the same care on the Windmill Hill site – hence its name. See the separate entry above for more information on that.

Costing £100 million to build and financed by the Kuwaiti-owned St Martin's Property Corporation, the site is indeed home to a range of stunning buildings, including Trigonos, headquarters of RWE (formerly National Power). In 1986 John Laing Construction Ltd laid the first brick for yet another notable business on Windmill Hill - PHH (now Arval) – a fleet car management company. PHH Europe PLC opened a half million-pound training centre at their HQ on Windmill Hill. More than 800 people worked for PHH in its glory days, managing over 120,000 vehicles. The training complex had the nickname 'PHH university' and ran a continuous programme of courses for its Swindon staff. In the early 2000s PHH became Arval, a subsidiary of BNP Paribas, Europe's largest bank, but retains its Swindon base on Windmill Hill.

The business park was developed on land which used to be Marsh Farm, see Chapter 7 on farms in West Swindon. The original farmhouse has been preserved and is now used as the site management office.

The West Swindon Centre – 1981
A Super Centre for a Super Bear

An ardent Super Ted fan, my daughter would've loved to see him flying in to the linchpin of West Swindon. As indeed would I, having a soft spot for the super hero bear and his spotty sidekick.

Roughly 3.2km from Swindon's town centre lies the West Swindon Centre. It's now generally known as the Asda Centre, as the company has gradually taken over most of the units within the building,

The 1968 Silver Book determined that a large shopping and commercial facility should be a key feature to the expansion westwards.

Soon after the first residents of the first 10,000 homes arrived in March 1976, joint land owners Thamesdown Borough Council and E H Bradley & Son invited interest from developers to undertake the design and build of the town's first large-scale out-of-town commercial centre, with free parking.

Some eight developers reached the final selection stage where each was required to prepare a detailed prospectus backed up by large-scale models. Of all the proposals received, one design stood out. From Linwood Ltd, it comprised a large building housing a main anchor store, a mall of small shops and external units arranged around a 'town square,' with a large garden centre in a separate glasshouse close by.

Building began in early 1980 and by October of that year, just in time for *Le Beaujolais Nouveau,* the French supermarket chain Carrefour opened in the main anchor store. It brought a touch of Gallic charm to West Swindon, with the in-store sommelier and delicatessen counter.

In the September 1981 edition of *Link* magazine, superstore general manager Peter Hartland outlined the Carrefour offer in a four-page pull-out. He stated, 'Supermarketing magazine describes Carrefour as "the most community-minded UK chain".' And in a sign of the times,

THE CARREFOUR SUPERSTORE AT THE WEST SWINDON SHOPPING CENTRE WILL OPEN AT 9.00 a.m. ON TUESDAY, OCTOBER 27, 1981.

P. Hartland
Store Director

carrefour/swindon

Dear Neighbours,

Through the kind co-operation of The Link, we have been invited to produce this supplement to your regular edition.

And since we are neighbours — and since you have probably been wondering what was to be the outcome of all the feverish activity on the site of The West Swindon Centre over the past year — we are fortunate to have this means of introducing ourselves and our shop to you.

Last autumn, we announced that the shopping centre and the Carrefour superstore would open at 9.00 a.m. on October 27, 1981 — and it will.

As you know, further phases to complete the full range of amenities, attractions and services around the centre are subsequently scheduled but the shopping centre for Linfood Ltd. and the Carrefour anchor store are ready on time — and that is so.

Both Linfood and Carrefour mark this tribute to Wimpeys, the main contractors, and all the subcontractors and workers on site, that is so.

Those readers, too, who have visited other district shopping centres will observe that this is one of Britain's most successfully thought-out Town Development Plans. People competent to make this judgment, indeed, are already saying it — which in turn is a tribute to the impetus, commitment and experience of the Thamesdown local authority.

So I really have no alibi, to run other than a first-class shop!

On this score, Carrefour has quite a good pedigree and Supermarketing magazine, for instance, were kind enough to describe Carrefour as "the most community-minded UK chain". And to the extent that you accept that housewives vote with their feet, people are also suggesting that Carrefour can claim to run the most popular self-service store in the country (actually, Carrefour/Bristol).

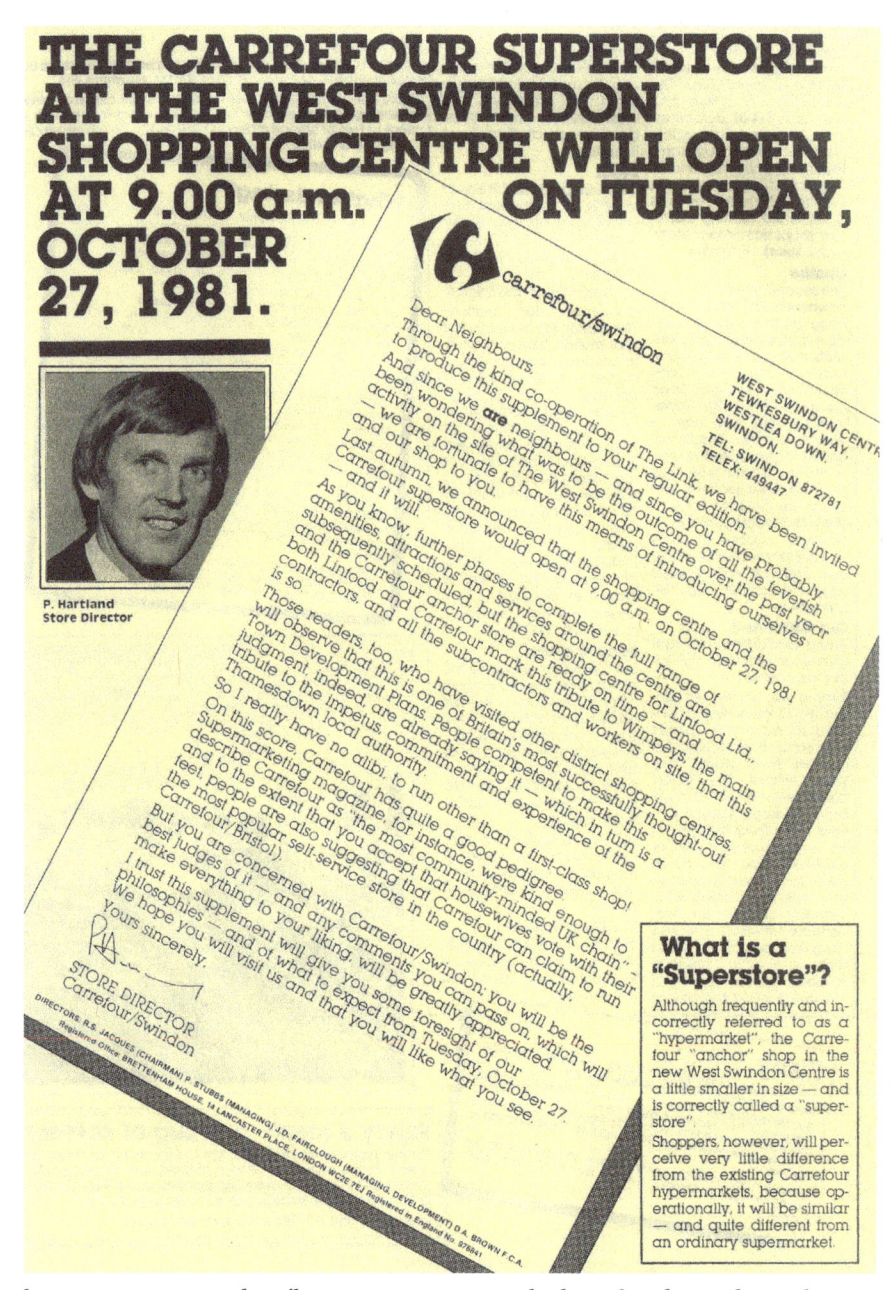

But you are concerned with Carrefour/Swindon: you will be the best judges of it — and any comments you can pass on, which will make everything to your liking, will be greatly appreciated.

I trust this supplement will give you some foresight of our philosophies — and of what to expect from Tuesday, October 27.

We hope you will visit us and that you will like what you see.

Yours sincerely,

STORE DIRECTOR
Carrefour/Swindon

What is a "Superstore"?

Although frequently and incorrectly referred to as a "hypermarket", the Carrefour "anchor" shop in the new West Swindon Centre is a little smaller in size — and is correctly called a "superstore".

Shoppers, however, will perceive very little difference from the existing Carrefour hypermarkets, because operationally, it will be similar — and quite different from an ordinary supermarket.

he went on to say that 'housewives vote with their feet by making the already open Carrefour in Bristol the most popular self-service store in the country.'

WHAT THE EYE DOESN'T SEE

The newly completed West Swindon Centre, before Link Centre and Shaw Ridge Leisure Park were built

The *Link* magazine supplement sets out how far ahead of the times the superstore was. There would be no impulse purchases at the checkouts, no sweets, razor blades or magazines. 'Checkouts are for checking-out, as quickly and efficiently as possible' it reads. Another selling point was the commitment to recycling cardboard delivery boxes and plastic shopping bags.

Gateway Stores later took over Carrefour in the UK, only to undergo takeover by the US corporation Walmart. In 2020 UK based retailer EG Group acquired the Asda chain.

It's doubtful that Super Ted would recognise it now.

The Toot and Whistle, Toothill – 1981

Built with second-hand bricks from Cheshire, the pub design by Michael Sasson featured a great amount of wood and wrought ironwork, and a bar front made from Mexican tea trays – the combined effect was that of a South American/Spanish *haçienda*. The first managers were Dave and Carol James.

Intended as a social and leisure centre for the community, special features included a children's room, skittle alley, darts, pool table and a large landscaped area for summer use.

In the run-up to the opening of West Swindon's first pub, Wessex Taverns ran a competition to find a name in the *Link* newsletter. More than 400 readers entered, with the children of Toothill Primary School emerging the winners with *Toot and Whistle*. The magazine reported that Wessex Taverns felt that *Toot and Whistle* said many different things and carried different meanings about Toothill, the railways and Swindon's historical links with them, the Toot Hill and Toot himself.

Adrian Stemp, pupil at Toothill Primary School provides an explanation: Toot is small with a green suit and a bobble on his hat. He has big black boots and they are magic. They can make him jump and

Recycled bricks in the newly built pub at Toothill

dance and he wears white and red socks. Toot is a little man and he lives around our school at Toothill.

The pub became the Toothill Tavern, but the business wasn't sustainable and the pub closed in 2017.

With a significant portion of the £1 million allocated by the National Lottery Big Local Fund to Toothill in 2010, the local committee negotiated a long lease for the site with Swindon Borough Council. Work on converting and extending the old building to become a community meeting and activity hub with a licensed area saw completion in the autumn of 2023.

The clockhouse at Shaw Village Centre

Shaw Village Centre – 1981

This village centre is not unlike those at Toothill and Freshbrook – though it doesn't have a community centre as each of those do. A site between the Village Inn and Holy Trinity Church remains empty for this purpose.

Yet Shaw has the widest range of different outlets and services of the four in West Swindon, thus it warrants some mention here. As well as the only veterinary practice in the area, there's also a senior's supported housing at George Tweed Gardens, a supermarket, a dental practice, chiropractic clinic, pharmacy and a takeaway outlet. Nearby the Ridge Green medical practice caters for the community's primary health requirements.

The Spectrum Building – AKA The Renault Building – 1982

Built as a vehicle component warehouse and distribution centre for the Renault car company, Madam La Lumiere, the then French Secretary of State for Consumer Affairs, performed the official opening on 15 June 1983.

Body parts on show in the Renault Building

    Designed by Sir Norman Foster, one of Britain's foremost contemporary architects, it's recognised as Britain's greatest exponent of ultra-modern design and simple streamlined structures. He's often referred to as the hero of high-tech, and proving that buildings don't have to be old or of traditional design to get recognition as special,

Juxtaposition: Two hundred year old conserved oak tree next to new steel construction

the Spectrum Building gained Grade II* listed status in 2013. Historic England cites its architectural interest as being a building of particular, early 1980s importance.

As part of his total design concept, Foster designed all the building's fixtures and fittings. This included free-standing office furniture and warehouse storage systems. He designed the glass tables with steel and aluminium legs for the reception area and cafeteria, to echo the design of the beams and mullions of the building itself.

The building won wide admiration. It won a Structural Steel award, a Civic Trust award and the *Financial Times* 'Architecture at Work' award – all in 1984. Then in 1986 it won the Constructa Prize for Industrial Architecture in Europe. And if all that were not excitement enough, 1985 saw the building feature in the James Bond film, *A View to a Kill,* thus giving it a place in cinema history.

Renault left the iconic building in 2001. It remained empty until 2005 when it gained a new name: Spectrum.

Over the years, the warehouse has seen use as a manufacturing plant for car seats and a tyre distribution facility. The glass fronted showroom was a Ford van dealership for a time and more recently an indoor children's play centre. The adjacent administration areas have undergone conversion into an indoor golf range and a workwear shop.

Freshbrook – The Cornflower - later The Windmill – 1982

The *Link* magazine of March 1982 reported good building progress on the new Whitbread Flowers pub due to open in October of that year. The

The Cornflower, as it was in the beginning

THE LINK

Special Freshbrook Issue
Sponsored By
Whitbread Flowers

OCTOBER 14th IS THE SUNSHINE DAY WHEN FRESHBROOK'S OWN PUB GOES ON TAP

THE CORNFLOWER

'The Cornflower' will officially open for trading at 7.00pm on Thursday, October 14th. Months of hard work have seen the pub take shape and the final result is one which does credit to all who have worked on this £300,000 project.

The interior is warm and friendly and is designed for community spirit. The pub offers customers the full range of Whitbread products, good food - and a taster is given overleaf, darts, pool and a skittle alley. There are conveniences specially designed for the disabled.

In addition, for those wishing to take the family out, there is a children's room with its own access.

We hope you will join us at the opening or call in to see your neighbours Terry and Jill Stapleton, the licensees, in the coming weeks.

Mike Peacock
Retail Manager, Whitbread Flowers

YOUR HOSTS

Terry and Jill Stapleton have six years experience in the trade. They were previously at The Tabard public house in Gloucester, another Whitbread Flowers property, where they gained a renowned reputation for their hospitality and excellence in pub food.

Both Terry and Jill were born and bred in Swindon and the period in Gloucester was one of their very infrequent journeys out of the Swindon area. Terry is a plumbing and heating engineer by trade but his adaptability to a friendly considerate licensee will not go unnoticed to 'The Cornflower' regulars.

The Link magazine Cornflower competition

article goes on to say that the interior will depict an old mill, complete with mill wheel and open fireplace. Facilities would also include a children's room, skittle alley, darts and pool along with home-cooked food at lunchtime and a cold buffet bar. As with the Toothill pub, the brewers ran a competition in the *Link* magazine to name the pub offering a barrel of beer, or its equivalent in cans, as a prize. Mr Ernest Kimber of Toothill suggested *The Cornflower*. He explained that, as a boy, he and his friends would walk the fields where Toothill and Freshbrook now stand. He said:

> the cornflower was a common sight in those days and it seemed right to give a modern landmark a rural feeling because this was all country not so long ago. I like trees and the fields and I'm a bit sorry to see them gone.

But the pub didn't retain its rural name for long. Come 1989, Whitbread Severn Inns were spending £250,00 on refurbishing the pub and decided the new look needed a new name. Thus, once more the *Link* magazine ran the competition. The rebrand saw the pub renamed *The Windmill* after the reconstruction and relocation of the Chiseldon windmill on the nearby business park.

But the proposal to rename *The Cornflower* failed to find universal favour. Though enthusiastic about the alterations, Grange Park resident Cathy Baker was less enamoured with the name change. She argued in *Link* magazine that the pub's original name gave a sense of what once had been where the pub now stands. She posited the importance of that in an area that was so very new, saying: 'I think a new name for *The Cornflower* will cause confusion. It will take years to overcome and, in the meantime, Freshbrook will have lost something of its past.'

Water Research Centre – 1982
An award-winning building designed by BDP Architects

The Water Research Centre in 1982

The building in 2023 livery

and originally a distinctive red colour, the water research centre sits on Frankland Road on the Blagrove industrial estate. Now rebranded as WRc the centre researches new ways to improve water and waste management systems around the world. The centre has more than 90 years of experience in helping regulators, industrial manufacturers, water and gas utility companies, and governmental, non-governmental and trade organisations.

In 2020, the environmental, engineering and technical services firm RSK Group acquired the independent Water Research Centre on Frankland Road and its subsidiary Cognica.

Toothill Community Centre – 1984

Swindon's mayor performed the opening ceremony for Toothill community centre on 22 September, 1984 – though it had been open for business since August of that year. At a cost of £250,000 the centre comprised the second of four similar facilities opened in 1984.

Following a design pattern for recently built community centres in other parts of Swindon, the building at Toothill centre included a hall with access to a kitchen, a large meeting room linked to the kitchen, a playgroup room with a covered terrace and its own toilets and a room for a licensed bar. Two small offices were also included. This was the same as at Freshbrook Community Centre.

See-through roof at Toothill community centre

The apex of the barrel roof lent itself to something unusual and, at the suggestion from the council's architect, twenty-eight students studying stained glass at the West Glamorgan institute of Higher Education in Swansea received invitations to visit West Swindon and submit proposals for the 5ft diameter space.

The centre's management committee, chose *Toothill Sunrise*, designed by Keith Gale. They felt this reflected various aspects of the local community and its environment. It depicts the new urban development set into Wiltshire countryside and references Swindon's railway heritage and the town's high-tech future as a major electronics employer. Behind the green 'hill' you can see the sun rising and casting out rays of hope and warmth for the future.

The Link Centre – 1985

Major leisure facilities in the western expansion to cater for the local population and a wider catchment across Swindon and its region was a key point in the Silver Book. The site in the first phase of the development was identified in the master plan of the early 1970s. Under the direction of Thamesdown Borough Council chief architect Ken Sherry, a team led by Nigel Honer undertook the design work and planning permission was granted in 1983.

Yet the £11 million project was not without its critics. Conservative opposition leader Angus Macpherson, quoted in the *Swindon Evening Advertiser*, felt the ice rink plan was going into 'cloud cuckoo land.' 'We are not against a social provision for the west of the borough but we feel they have gone too far,' he declared. He also criticised the idea that the ice rink would not only cater for Thamesdown residents but everyone between Reading and Bristol as well. 'It is questionable whether Thamesdown ratepayers should provide facilities for as wide an area as that,' he said.

The building features a mast and cable-stayed construction somewhat similar to the nearby Renault Centre designed by Sir Norman Foster and Partners. Whereas the roof of the latter was supported by multiple pylons within the structure, the Link Centre required large spaces without internal supports to incorporate an ice rink, a two and half court sports hall including the largest climbing wall in England, swimming pool, and the largest library in Swindon.

The Link Centre site before building started

Building Link Centre: the central pylons being erected in early 1984, with Shaw Ridge and construction of the Tewkesbury Way bridge towards Shaw underway.

Building Link Centre: the structure exposed before the walls went up

Further, to be found inside would be an arts and craft studio with performance space, a snooker room, a health suite with sauna and jacuzzi. There also used to be a community centre on the first floor comprising a large hall, a pre-school room, two meeting rooms and four small offices for local groups.

The user requirements meant four very large columns built at the centre of the structure with pillars arranged around the perimeter of the building supporting the lightweight roof. Construction commenced in June 1983 but soon hit problems as the foundation drilling went down and down into the clay ground for which the Swindon area is well known. Huge quantities of material were brought up without finding a strong enough layer of rock. A secret report to the council identified the need for an increase in the budget. It even suggested abandoning the project. Savings were made on internal fittings and more money was poured into the foundation piling to ensure the stability of the structure.

The design set out to be as energy efficient as possible with heat generated by the ice-rink refrigeration system being used to warm the swimming pool and the internal areas. Another innovation was making the large central mall a public space accessible without restriction during

The swimming pool in 1986, looking towards St Peter's Church, before the building of Shaw Ridge Leisure Park

1985, the first visitors lining up ready to try ice skating

opening hours. But the Link Centre became a magnet for some groups, particularly in cold weather, resulting at times in disorder, vandalism and disruption to the running of the centre.

This policy was dropped within a couple of years and, with clearer but low-key security the building started to realise its full potential as a flexible centre offering a wide range of not only sports competitions, excellence training and recreation, but also public meetings, learning events, performances and concerts.

Ground-breaking in its day, architectural and sports journals described the centre as the most comprehensive development of its kind

The Link Centre was named after competition run by Thamesdown Borough Council in 1984. The winners received gift vouchers from Councillor Tony Mayer, chairman of the council's Arts & Recreation Committee, second from left. The winners were young resident Sharon McColl, front, and the volunteers who produced the Link community newsletter, from left Nick Jansen, Janice Oliver, Roger Ogle and Eric Edwards (Swindon Advertiser)

in Britain. For several years Swindon's recreational provision of the Oasis Centre complemented by the Link Centre was regarded as the best in the south of England. The Mayor of Swindon Harry Garrett took to the ice rink after performing the opening ceremony in April 1985. The other facilities opened in phases until the centre was fully-functional by July. It was an instant hit with an estimated one million visitors attracted to the Link Centre in its first operational year.

The naming of the centre was something of a fix after the borough director of recreation approached the coordinator of the, then volunteer run, *Link* newsletter about naming the centre through a competition in late 1994. This duly took place and 13-year-old Sharon McColl from Old Town and volunteers who produced the *Link* were announced as the winners.

A plaque unveiled by Mayor Harry Garrett in 1985, still viewable at the entrance to the Link Centre, dedicates the building to skaters, players, leapers, loungers, neighbours, climbers, bathers, actors, watchers, writers. workers, potters, champions, craftsmen and readers.

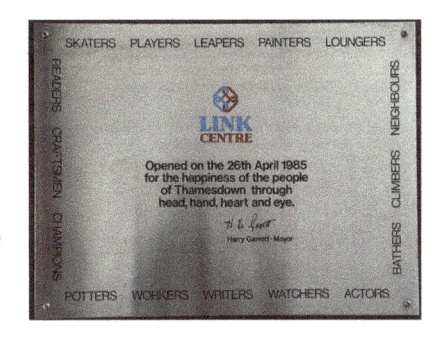

In 2013 Swindon Borough Council leased the building to leisure charity GLL who rationalised and simplified the facilities on offer. The council had converted the arts centre into a gym in 2010. But under new management the community centre was converted into a much larger gym. Further, in the sports hall they replaced the climbing wall, funded by a £74,000 lottery grant, with a huge trampoline park.

Swindon Borough Council continue to manage the library.

St Peter's Catholic Church, Eastleaze – 1985

The congregation of St Peter's can thank Rev. Liam O'Driscoll for driving the project to provide a place of Catholic worship. Before its construction, members met in various locations, including Toothill's shared church, local schools and even Fr O'Driscoll's converted garage.

On 22 February 1985, Bishop Alexander laid the church's foundation stone, and the building was ready for use at Midnight Mass at the Christmas of the same year. A parish centre and presbytery were built at the same time. The church was designed by the architectural firm of Ivor Day, O'Brien, Stephens, and five stained-glass panels by John Potter were added in 2000 and 2007.

The website Taking Stock: Catholic Churches of England and Wales gives a detailed description of the design, the sculptures, artwork, furnishings and stained-glass windows within the building. Colour and enrichment in the church come from the furnishings. According to sources, there is one item of notable antiquity. That being an octagonal stone font of possible late 15th-century date with uncertain provenance, although it has now been identified as coming from Stoke Wake in Dorset. Another corner holds a statue of St Peter – an 1890s copy of the famous bronze statue in St Peter's in Rome. Yet another corner houses the 1905 Griffen and Stroud pipe organ that came from Marlborough United Reformed Church.

The Chinese Experience – 1989

In the mid-1980s a consortium of Chinese businessmen approached Thamesdown Borough Council for a site where they could build a very large restaurant. As the development of Roughmoor was starting to take place and the excavations of Peatmoor Lagoon had commenced, borough council planners had just the right place.

The brief to the developers and their architects was to make the building Chinese enough to make a strong statement overlooking the eastern end of the lake, next to Mead Lake, which would later join West Swindon to the development in the north of the town. Swindon practice, Wyvern Architects took on the task of bringing a touch of the Orient to the western expansion.

Built around a steel frame, with brick and timber-clad external walls, the pagoda sported the traditional Chinese colours of reds, greens and yellow. At the time no-one in the UK made colourful glazed tiles of the right shape. An overseas search sourced that element of the design in Japan. The roof decorations of dragons, lions, fish and other animals found decorating oriental buildings, came from Hong Kong. Meanwhile, the hand-painted decorative panels that formed a continuous frieze around the walls came from Taiwan.

The small, open-sided pagoda on an island opposite the main building was imported in fibreglass sections and assembled on concrete foundations.

In March 1989 Councillor Jim Cordon,

March 18th 1989, the Mayor of Swindon Jim Cordon with Lawrence Lee and his business associates at the start of work on the Chinese Experiance

Mayor of Thamesdown, drove a digger to open up the site. He also carried out the opening ceremony with the Union flag and the flag of the Chinese People's Republic flying side by side. What's more, according to a West Swindon resident present at the opening ceremony, flags were not the only thing flying. Sparks also flew from the setting off of an over-abundance of Chinese firecrackers that had guests fleeing. At the time

The Chinese Experience and the island pagoda, both now hidden by vegetation

the Mayor Cordon said: 'I enjoyed the experience of driving the digger, in particular because the project is another innovation for Swindon – we are always doing new things.'

When it opened the £1.6million project enjoyed status as the UK's largest Chinese restaurant.

Back in 2004, Swindon Borough Council (SBC) published a dry-as-dust-document called *Buildings of Significant Local Interest*. In it, they categorize *The Chinese Experience* as a building that has: 'landmark quality or contributes to the character of an area or the quality of recognisable spaces, by virtue of its function, location, age, design or features.' All of which says nothing about how exciting and innovative this building was in its day.

The pagoda on the island in the lagoon, still standing after nearly 35 years (Casey Slade)

The Chinese Experience closed in the 1990s and after several years unused when there was significant vandalism, the restaurant reopened as Pagoda Palace, later the Oriental Buffet, and is now the Hongxin Oriental Buffet.

Delta Tennis Centre – 1989

Here's another example of Swindon's ambitious efforts to create sporting and leisure opportunities for all. The steel-framed building accommodating four indoor courts plus two outside courts was officially opened on 26 April 1989 by the late Diana, Princess of Wales. Two weeks of have-a-go sessions to introduce tennis to people of all ages preceded her visit.

The skeleton tennis centre taking shape next to Welton Road

The tennis centre on Welton Road, Westlea has continued to offer tennis for all, as well as opportunities to progress to competition excellence. It's now managed on a long lease from Swindon Borough Council by leisure charity GLL.

Oak House, Rivermead – 1989

If there is a building in West Swindon shrouded in mystery, Oak House is it. Surrounded by tall security fencing, its blank, black face fronts Mead Way.

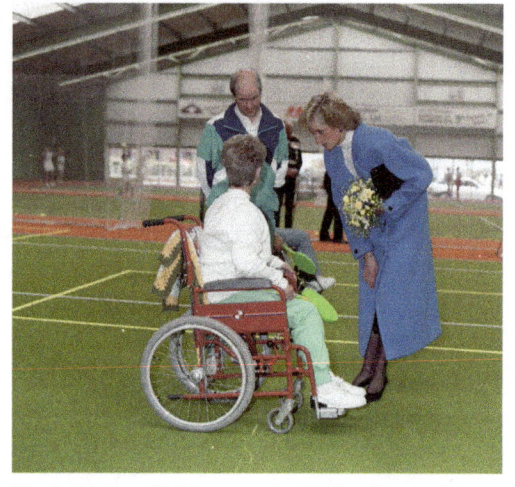

The Princess of Wales meets a Delta Tennis Centre user with centre manager Neil Allen in 1989. (Richard Wintle, Calyx Multimedia)

Oak House was built as a data and payment processing centre for the Department of Social Security. Inside were administration offices and giant mainframe computers holding the details of millions of benefit claimants. Dozens of civil servants operated printing machines and despatched unemployment cheques, income support books and pension voucher books.

The mysterious building viewed by thousands of passing drivers daily

A rationalisation of services and the move to sending benefit payments by direct bank transfer rendered the building redundant in the early 2000s. After more than twenty years standing empty, Oak House and the large site it occupies faces an unknown future.

Shaw Ridge Leisure Park – 1990
The front page of the December 1989 edition of *Link* magazine reported the Mayor of Swindon Ken Savage taking controls of the JCB to start construction, after Thamesdown Council's planning committee had given permission for a multi-screen cinema, a bowling alley, night club, hotel, a pub, a themed bar and a fast-food restaurant surrounding a very large car park. The mayor said he was particularly glad to see ten-pin bowling return to Swindon after twenty years.

Bryan Smith of Carter Commercial Developments, the company behind the project, paid tribute to the officers and members of the

The Shaw Ridge Leisure Park site before construction commenced

council who had demonstrated great professionalism and enthusiasm for the project. He said: 'They laid down time-scales and have stuck with them. We in the private sector appreciate this; the Shaw Ridge Leisure Park is a good example of partnership between a public authority and a private developer.' He added the park would be very attractive to people who live close by and those from further afield. 'I live in Bristol and I often bring my family to enjoy what Swindon has. It's very impressive and Shaw Ridge is being used as a model for other developments in other parts of the country.'

John Fisher, manager of the adjacent Link Centre said: 'The cinema, Superbowl, restaurants and night club will complement the Link Centre. With its four-star hotel and the Hotel Ibis near Delta Tennis Centre, Swindon is going to be a major tourist attraction for families who want to take an active weekend break. As a resident of West Swindon, the area is becoming even more attractive to live in.'

2004: Westlea Primary School youngsters visiting the Diana Dors statue designed by John Clinch and installed in June 1991

The leisure park opened the end of November 1990 and became extremely busy throughout the decade with people bowling, strutting their stuff in Cairo's Nightclub, enjoying the Americana at Pinkertons Café-Bar-Restaurant, as well as crowding out Pizza Hut.

The MGM 7-screen cinema opened with a fun day and tours behind the scenes in April 1991. *Robin Hood: Prince of Thieves, Terminator 2: Judgment Day, Home Alone,* and *Teenage Mutant Ninja Turtles* pulled the crowds in huge numbers. Over the next few years, Princess Diana and her young sons, princes William and Harry, discreetly visited the MGM cinema to enjoy age-appropriate films. William and Harry also attended the cinema in their teenage years.

June 1991 saw the unveiling of a larger than life statue honouring Swindon cinematic heartthrob Diana Dors outside the MGM cinema. She's portrayed from her 1956 film *Yield to the Night*. Some of the names on the front doors across the park have changed, but Diana Dors continues to gaze out across West Swindon.

Arclite House – 1999

The western development master plan allocated land for employment on the edge of West Swindon; Hillmead is the only one between the housing areas. Arclite House is situated on a prime site on the edge of Peatmoor Lagoon.

In contrast to the industrial boxes at Hillmead, the *Architect's Journal* describes Arclite thus: 'An experimental design of curved glazing and playfully complex interior structures for a Swindon call centre.' The sun-facing side of the building features a black wall of insulated heat-absorbing material. The north side facing the lagoon is largely composed of glass with solar shades on the interior. An array of architectural, environmental and workplace awards followed the opening in 1999, including the best large office award FX Magazine International Interior Design.

WHAT THE EYE DOESN'T SEE

The beached torpedo next to Peatmoor Lagoon

    The £6 million structure was commissioned by Cellular Operations, the Ford Motor Company mobile communications arm, providing support to the firm, its dealers and customers. Architect Richard Hywel-Evans had the brief to create an iconic building – one that would put the tenants on the map and onto everyone's lips. A further important criterion was the creation of a humane working environment that would attract and retain staff.

    Ford Magic, providers of assistance to customers with disabilities, rented part of the building. That aside, the building featured employee relaxation areas, themed washrooms and a fountain activated by operation of the lift.

Dubbed the glass cigar, the torpedo or the Zeppelin building, it was completed in under ten months and opened in 1999. Yet the nuances of working in a pleasant environment were lost on the local media and residents who objected to the ultra-modern look. Nevertheless, the planning committee, in keeping with its brave outlook, disagreed and passed the plans.

A few months later the site found itself once more enveloped in controversy when Cellular Operations and Richard Hywel-Evans proposed an equally futuristic glass fronted capsule with a lightweight roof as a café on the very edge of the lagoon. This would have been open to both company staff and the public, but it would have meant the realignment of the footpath around the lagoon. Petitions were raised in advance of the borough's planning control committee at the end of January 2000. There were 417 in favour for and 207 against. A Peatmoor resident saw the café as another totally alien structure which would detract from the peace and tranquillity enjoyed by local residents and fishermen.

Yet, Councillor Peter Mallinson welcomed the proposal saying:

> It would have been easy for Cellular Operations to have proposed a concrete box for its headquarters like so many other buildings in Swindon. We must congratulate them on their innovation which will draw interest and attention to the area. The cafe will benefit local residents, people from across the town who visit the lagoon and the anglers who fish there.

The council planning committee ruled in favour of Cellular Operations, but the project didn't progress any further as different corporate priorities started to emerge. Despite its award-winning status and success, in 2003 Ford sold Cellular Operations and its 360,000 customers to Vodafone. There were hopes of the Swindon site continuing to operate, but it wasn't long before Arclite and the 470 people working there found themselves declared surplus to requirements. After languishing empty for several years, a 2012 refurbishment saw the building split into three large units. Excalibur IT mobile communications occupied the upper floors and in 2015 the Princess Royal paid a visit to the award-winning company.

The proposed Cellular Operations cafe that was never built on the banks of Peatmoor Lagoon

    Jaywing brand awareness call centre occupied the largest part of the building, whilst the smallest unit on the ground floor has been empty since Cellular Operations closed. In 2021 all the tenants had moved out and another refurbishment commenced.

West Swindon Schools

Shaw Ridge Primary School 1985 and 2009
First built in 1985, the original school had the name, Shaw Ridge County Primary School. That incarnation of the school lasted until 2009, when the current building replaced it, built to cater for the larger intake as a result of the closure of Salt Way Primary school.

Aside from its unusual circular design, this school boasts a couple of other features worthy of mention. In 2020, during the Covid 19 pandemic, the school used the site of the original school to create an educational environmental space for the children and a place for people living in the area to benefit from.

The school asked the pupils to suggest names for the garden but, as the headteacher Sally Cowell said, 'Unity Garden felt like the perfect choice, because at that time we felt like we needed to be united against this common pandemic.'

WHAT THE EYE DOESN'T SEE

The garden has different areas including a beach area where children can learn about coastal erosion, a pond, a vegetable patch, raised flower beds for flowers and bulbs and an orchard area. Complementing the beach area is an art installation by West Swindon artist, Billy Beaumont. He explained that the friends of Shaw Ridge school approached him to ask if it were possible for him to create an ocean effect on an old playground at the school. Their thinking being that it would make a perfect finish to the community beach area.

Peatmoor Primary School

Shortly after the first children arrived at the new school in September 1999, a collection of brightly, larger than life, coloured pencils was installed in the roundabout in the school car park. In 2008 the pencils received national exposure when they appeared on the December page of the UK Roundabout Appreciation Society calendar. In 2016, staff from Nationwide HQ sharpened the pencils up by giving them a sanding down and repainting them.

Toothill Primary School – 1979 and 2008

As West Swindon's oldest primary school, Toothill primary had been built on two levels to designs suitable to the era. Over the years, an increasing number of mobile classrooms were erected to cater for the demands from the early families setting up home in the area.

In the Swindon Borough Council school's reorganisation of 2005, Toothill was selected to have a modern replacement which opened in September 2008. The £4.5m building included solar panels to heat water and a green roof of sedum and other low-growing pollinator friendly plants.

Well known TV personality Kevin

Kevin McCloud with Toothill Primary headteacher Martin Cowell and school councillor Kornelia Konwa

Princess Anne officially opened Greendown School in March 1987. She is pictured watching gymnasts Martina Flaherty and Clancy MacMullen with headteacher Ian Matthews, right, and Roger Ogle, chair of governors. Photo: Richard Wintle, Calyx Multimedia

McCloud visited the following year to officially open the school and talk to pupils about the flowers and vegetables they'd been growing throughout the first year of the new building. In 2013 the school became part of the Academies Enterprise Trust and reopened as Hazelwood Academy.

Greendown Community School/Lydiard Park Academy

After much discussion in the early 1980s, Wiltshire County Council, still the education authority for Swindon, finally succumbed to pressure for a secondary school in West Swindon. The £1.5 million expenditure was the first new secondary school built in the county for twenty years, and the first purpose-built community school. Greendown Community School opened in Grange Park in 1986.

Taking its name from nearby Greendown Copse on the edge of Lydiard Park, the school had a specific brief to serve the area by opening its facilities to adult evening classes, community organisations and sports clubs.

Greendown School in 2000, with Link Centre in the middle distance and Swindon town centre beyond

Princess Anne formally opened the school on 23 March 1987. Before unveiling a plaque to mark the occasion, she toured the school to meet pupils, parents and staff, and called into the playgroup using the community hall.

In 2007 Greendown was designated a sport, maths and computing specialist school. With the accompanying funding, the school bought a gym, replaced the original Astro-turf sports surface, upgraded all the computers and installed interactive whiteboards in every mathematics classroom.

The autumn of 2010 saw Greendown become the second Swindon school to open a Special Resource Provision for pupils with autism.

In 2011 the school adopted academy status as the founding member of The Park Academies Trust. Since then the Trust has grown with the addition of another Swindon secondary school, Abbey Park School in North Swindon, and three primaries, Red Oaks, Orchid Vale and Bridlewood. Further, Highworth's Warneford school joined the Trust in September 2023. That will make the Multi Academy Trust the largest in terms of Swindon pupils in the town.

The sixth form opened in September 2014 with the vision of improving the percentage of pupils who go on to higher education. The sixth form has met this aspiration with double the percentage of pupils going on to university compared to the rest of Swindon.

Lost buildings

Building on the green fields to the west of Swindon has been the key feature since the early 1970s. But there's also been change. What follows are some buildings worth mentioning that have been and gone – one way and another.

Close to Mead Way, the Westlea Campus office complex appeared in the mid-1980s. But the early 2000s saw it demolished to make way for housing and a small supermarket.

West Swindon once had its own large police station, opposite Westlea Fire Station which is still in service. Demolition took place in 2005 to make way for housing.

The bright yellow Anchor Butter cold storage, packaging and distribution centre at Blagrove was a landmark to all passing on Great Western Way and the M4, until tree growth hid it from view. Built in

WHAT THE EYE DOESN'T SEE

Building on the green fields to the west of Swindon has been the key feature since the early 1970s. But there has also been change. Here are some examples of buildings that have been and gone.

Close to Mead Way, the Westlea Campus office complex was built in the mid-1980s. and demolished in the early 2000s to make way for housing and a small supermarket.

West Swindon once had its own large police station, opposite Westlea Fire Station which is still in service. Demolition took place in 2005 to make way for housing.

Anchor operations in Swindon closed in 2002 following the takeover of New Zealand Milk by European dairy company Arla. Whilst the Anchor logo is no longer on show, the building has been reconfigured and continues to be used by a variety of small and large businesses.

Blagrove employment area was the first UK base for major technology company Motorola ECID. It arrived in the black glass and red steel structure 1989, one of four buildings eventually occupied in the town. At one time 3,000 people were employed and in 1995 the company was awarded the Queen's Award for Export Achievement. Princess Anne visited the plant in 1996. By the early 2000s intense competition in the mobile phone market forced rationalisation across the telecommunications sector. The building was vacated in the middle of the decade and this was followed by demolition. The site is now used as showrooms and workshops for luxury cars.

1980 as the UK plant for New Zealand butter imports, in its heyday almost 1,000 people worked there.

Anchor operations in Swindon closed in 2002 following the takeover of New Zealand Milk by European dairy company Arla. Whilst the Anchor logo is no longer on show, the building underwent reconfiguration. It's now used by a variety of small and large businesses.

The Blagrove employment area was the first UK base for major technology company Motorola ECID (European Cellular Infrastructure Division). It arrived in the black glass and red steel structure in 1989, One of four buildings they occupied in the town. At one time 3,000 people worked across the town and in 1995 the company received the Queen's Award for Export Achievement. The year 1996 saw the Royal seal of approval when Princess Anne visited the Motorola manufacturing plant at Blagrove.

By the early 2000s intense competition in the mobile phone market forced rationalisation across the telecommunications sector. The company vacated the building in the middle of the decade and it was later demolished. The site is now occupied by luxury car dealerships for Ferrari and Porsche.

And to End …

Three tall, strange figures sit
Like time-travellers from the future
(Westwords)
Jon Buck's sculpture in Westlea, It was later moved next to the ponds at West Swindon Centre

If this book had a particular aim, it would be to puncture the common perception that West Swindon is yet another urban sprawl with nothing to commend it – either past or present. Except, perhaps, proximity to the M4.

So, it's our hope that, in flicking through the pages of this volume, you've seen that, beyond the 1970s and 1980s housing there are a great many unseen stories. Stories that stretch back to, if not the dawn of time, then not so far from it.

And if there are stories here - then there are stories everywhere. All you have to do is look for them.

Last lines from the 1999 West Swindon Long Poem, *Westwords*

A lone fox out hunting
Scavenging through litter
Without a natural habitat now
Calls out in answer
To the bleary saxophone hoot
Of a late car or the wailing siren
Of an ambulance or the police
Speeding towards the distant hum of the M4.

And in Westlea Park
Three tall, strange figures sit
Like time-travellers from the future
Casually relaxing on a stone wall
Overlooking the pond
Looking into the pond
Looking into the future
Night after night
Guarding a time capsule
Watching everything that passes
Half-smiles on their timeless faces
As if they know all that has happened
All that is happening
And all that will happen.
But they will not tell.

A conclusion written by twenty-eight students from Greendown Community School (now Lydiard Park Academy) and pupils from Brook Field, Freshbrook, Salt Way, Shaw Ridge, Toothill, Tregoze and Westlea primary schools and Oliver Tomkins Junior School.

Acknowledgements

The authors wish to express their thanks to their sources of information:

- The outstanding repository of local and family history that is Swindon's local studies team, who you'll find in the central library.
- *Swindon: a study for further expansion*, 1968 (Swindon Expansion Project Joint Committee).
- *Swindon Further Expansion. Report of the joint technical team on selection of the first area, Toothill*, 1971.
- Michael Harloe, *Swindon: a town in transition*, 1975.
- Martin Boddy, et al, *City for the 21st Century? Globilisation, planning and urban change in contemporary Britain*, 1997.
- Bernard Phillips, *The Archaeology of the Borough of Swindon* (2021).
- The Lydiard archives. An ever-growing online repository featuring portraits, furniture and architecture, as well as letters, photographs, memories and manuscripts. Find it here: https://www.thelydiardarchives.org.uk
- *Swindon Link Magazine*
- *Swindon Advertiser*
- *Thamesdown News*
- Victoria & Albert Museum, London, for inclusion of artefacts in the photograph on p. 69.
- National Library of Scotland (https://maps.nls.uk/) on p. 87.
- Ordnance Survey, on p. 104.

The authors have made every attempt to seek permission for copyright material used in this book. But if they've inadvertently used copyright material without permission/acknowledgement they offer profuse apologies and will make the necessary corrections at the first opportunity. Finally, they'd like to thank the publisher John Chandler, without whom this would undoubtedly have been a much thinner volume.

Index of Names and Places

Abbey Meads 14
Abbey Park School 146
Academies Enterprise Trust 145
AEthelstan 35
Akers, Elizabeth 94
Alcatel (Alcatel-Lucent) 57
Aldi 104
Alexander, Bishop 130
Alfred, king 26, 35
Alfred of Marlborough 63
Allen, Neil 134
Alpine Close 29
Americana, The 137
Anchor Butter 146, 148-9
Andover (Hants) 47
Antiock's Well 89
Apley (Shropshire) 80
Applewood Court 27
Arclite House 138, 141
Arla 148-9
Arle Court (Glos) 96
Arval 112
Asda 113, 115
Ashley, Anthony 96
Ashley-Cooper, Cropley 97
Atherton, Atalya 59
Attwood, Carleton 50-1
Aubrey, John 89
Australia 84

Badcock, Joses 94
Bailey's Farm 96, 103
Baird Close 30
Baker, Cathy 122
Bakers Mead 96
Baldwin, Samuel 78
Barbury Castle 7

Barnfield Bridge 49
Barnfield Treatment Works 48
Barrett Bristol Ltd 27, 29
Bawden, Mike 50
BDP Architects 122
Beauchamp, Margaret 64, 78
Beaumaris Road 26-7
Beaumont, Billy 65, 143
Becket, Thomas 81
Berkshire Drive 30
Bermejo, Vega 55
Bevan, Frances 111
Bissex, Rebecca 58
Blacklands 96
Blagrove 14, 42, 84, 86-8, 92, 123, 148-9
Blount, Elizabeth 77
BMW 69, 73
BNP Paribas 112
Bodiam Drive 91
Bolingbroke family 9, 30-1, 44, 67, 69, 73-4, 84, 87-8, 93, 95, 101, 103; see also St John
Boulton, Tom and Elizabeth 111
Bowood House 68
Bradley, E H 15, 27, 113
Bradon Forest 25, 40, 97
Bradon Forest School 20
Bramptons estate 35, 103
Breadmore, William 111
Bridlewood School 146
Brize Norton (Oxon) 22
Brook (Brookhouse) Farm 82, 93-4, 111
Brook Field School 19, 151
Buck, Jon 51-2, 150
Butt, Thomas Packer 96, 101
Butts Road, Chiseldon 108
Buxton, Sir Robert 97

Cairo's Nightclub 137
Canterbury, Archbishop 77
Carey, Francis 88
Carrefour 113–15
Carter, Henry 105, 111
Carter Commercial Developments 135
Cartwright Drive (Way) 30, 52, 107
Charles II, king 31
Charolais Drive 30
Charterhouse School 26, 86, 88–90
Cheltenham (Glos) 47
Cheshire 116
Chesters Play Area 50
Chinese Experience 42, 131–3
Chiseldon 88, 108–10, 112, 122
Clarendon, Lord 84
Clark, John 103
Clarke, Jonas 88, 94
Clarke Drive 30
Clarke Homes 30
Cleeves Close 74
Clinch, John 54, 137
Coate Water 42
Cognica 123
Cole, Jane 86–7
Cole, Sarah and Stephen 97
Cole, Stephen Edward 98
Cole family 103
Colliers Row 105
Compton, William and family 86
Conisborough 26
Constructa Prize 120
Cordon, Jim 51, 131, 133
Corsham 98
Corton Crescent 39
Cowell, Martin 144
Cowell, Sally 142
Cox, Jenny 47
Creeches Farm 67
Creighton, Kim 62
Cricklade 13, 47–8, 111

Davies, Terry and Theresa 16
Day, Ivor 130
Deerhurst Way 18
DEFRA 69
Delta Tennis Centre 133–4, 137

Devizes 101
Diana, Princess of Wales 31, 133
Dickinson, Gordon 58–9
Domesday Book 104
Dore 86
Dore, Richard 91–2
Dors, Diana 54–5, 137–8
Dors-Lake, Jason 54–5
Dunger, Claudine 61
Dunwich Drive 17

Eastleaze 14–5, 19, 38, 83, 101, 130
Edington Close 26
Edwards, Eric 129
Edwards, Walter 98
Egypt 92
Elcombe, Wroughton 86
Eldene 14
Ellandun, Battle 35
Ellison, James 88
Elmore, Pat 51
English Heritage 69
Enion, Henry 103
Ermin Street 33
Ewyas, Barony 63

Fairford (Glos) 22
Farndale, Louise 58
Ferrari 149
Finch-Crisp, Sarah 72
Fisher, John 137
Fitchew, Elizabeth 94
Flaherty, Martina 144
Ford Motor Co (Ford Magic) 120, 139, 141
Foster, Sir Norman 118–9, 125
Fox Wood 27
Frankland Road 123
Freshbrook 14, 18–20, 22, 27, 29–30, 38-9, 52, 82–3, 85, 117, 120, 122, 124, 151
Furnese, Anne and Sir Robert 63
Furuta, Hideo 52

Gaia, goddess 46
Gale, Keith 55–6, 125
Gardner, Paul 77
Garrett, Harry 20, 129
Gerard Walk 29

GLL charity 61, 129, 134
Gloucester 58, 63, 78
Gloucestershire 26, 29, 96
Goddard Arms Hotel 94, 103
Gooch, Sir Daniel 10
Grandison family 64, 80
Great Shelfinch 93
Greendown Community School 7, 20–1, 28, 144–6, 151
Griffen and Stroud organ 131
Groundwell Ridge 14, 34

Hagbourne Copse 42, 44
Haines, Mary and Mary Gladys 98
Hampshire Close 29
Harris, Lewis 58
Hart, Allen 102
Hartland, Peter 113
Hastings, Battle 36
Hay Lane 30, 35, 74
Haydon Wick 13–14
Hazelwood Academy 145
Heard, Clive and Amanda 32
Henry VIII, king 29
Henry of Huntingdon 35
Hereford, Earl of 63
Highgrove Area 27
Highland Close 29
Highworth 146
Hillmead 138
Hinton, Mark 58
Hinton Cottages 105
Hirsch, Andrea 100
Hiscock, Edward 67
Holbein, Hans 29
Holbeins development 28–9
Holinshed Place (Raphael) 29
Holland, Matt 100
Hollick, William 105
Holloway, Anthony 61
Honer, Nigel 125
Hong Kong 131
Hongxin Oriental Buffet 133
Hook, Robert Henry and Walter Charles 102
Hook Farm 66, 83
Hook Street 21, 29–30
Hughes, James 97

Hughes, Robert 96
Humphries, Abraham 88
Hungerford, Lucy 78
Huntingdon, Henry of 35
Hywel-Evans, Richard 139–40

Ibis, Hotel 137
Idovers Drive 27
Intel Corporation 69
Isis, cult 34

Jansen, Nick 129
Japan 10, 131
Jaywing 141
Jefferies, Percy 16
Jenkins, Sir Simon 81
John, David Murray 67-9
Jones, john Hedley 98

Kiln Park 33, 39, 92
Kimber, Ernest 122
King, Olive 89
King, Richard Dore 91–2
King family 87, 88, 92
Kingsbridge Hundred 84
Knowles family 80
Konwa, Kornelia 144

Laing Construction 112
Lansdown, Lord 68
Larkin, William 78
Lavington, T (auctioneer) 101
Lawe, John 92
Lee, Lawrence 131
Leighton, Anne 78
Leighton, Thomas 80
Lewis, Tim 56
Liden 14
Linge, Abraham van 80
Link Centre 18, 22, 61, 115, 125-6, 128-9, 137, 145
Link magazine (newsletter) 21, 113, 115-16, 120-2, 135
Linwood Ltd 113
Little Toot Hill 89
Littlecote Close 27
Livesey, Julie 52–3
London 9–10, 78, 85

Lower Shaw Farm 82, 97-100, 103-4
Lower Studley Farm 88
Lumiere, Madam La 118
Lydiard Brook 41
Lydiard Estate (including Church, House and Park) 6, 9, 26, 30-2, 35-6, 44, 60-1, 63-75, 78, 80-1, 83, 87-8, 93-6, 103-4, 107
Lydiard Green 28
Lydiard Millicent 13, 28, 87, 93, 95-6, 98, 101, 103, 106
Lydiard Park Academy 7, 21, 60, 145,151
Lydiard Tregoz 34, 77, 83-4, 86-7, 93, 95-6, 102-3, 109
Lyneham 22

Macgregor, John E M 67
MacMullen, Clancy 144
Macpherson, Angus 125
Mallet, John Lewis 93
Mallinson, Peter 140
Mannington 14, 16, 24-5, 83, 86, 91-2
Maple Heights 28
Markenfield 16, 26
Marlborough 101, 131
Marlborough, Alfred of 63
Marlborough, Duke of 31
Marney Road 29
Marsh Farm 35, 109, 112
Matthews, Ian 144
Mayer, Tony 54, 129
McCloud, Kevin 144-5
McColl, Sharon 129
McLean Homes 27, 28
Mead, The 93
Mead Lake 131
Mead Way 26, 42, 53, 134, 146-7
Melmouth, Thmas 89
Menzies, Michael 30
Mercer, Fergus 60
Mercia, kingdom 35
MGM cinema 137-8
Middleleaze 15, 19, 30, 59, 94-5
Midland & S W Junction Railway 47
Millbrook Primary School 19
Moody, Connor 58
Moore, Marcus 7
Moore, Nick 57

Motorola ECID 148-9
Mouldon Hill 13, 48
Munoz, Patricio Marin 60

NAAFI 92
Nahal, Mandeep 58
Nationwide Building Society 143
New Zealand 148-9
Newbury (Berks) 12
Newbury, battle 80
Newmarket (Cambs) 73
Newport Street Chapel, Swindon 91
Nexus 52
Nicaragua 60, 62
Nine Elms 15, 83, 105, 107, 111
North Swindon 34, 57, 146
North Wilts Canal 9, 48
North Wilts Herald 67, 104
Northampton, Earl of 86

Oak House 29, 134-5
Oaksey 94
Oasis Centre 129
Ocotal (Nicarague) 60, 62
Ogle, Roger 129, 144
Old Shaw Lane 104-7, 111
Oliver, Janice 129
Oliver Tomkins School 18, 85, 151
Osman, Jane and Thomas 91
Overton 103
O'Driscoll, Rev Liam 130

Parr, Katherine 29
Parsons, Wilfred and Mrs 92
Pears, Harold 94
Peatmoor 15-6, 19, 25, 32, 96, 140
Peatmoor Copse 39-40, 43
Peatmoor Lagoon 16, 40-3, 46, 131, 138-9, 141
Peatmoor Primary School 143
Penhill 16
Perry, Richard 58
Pevsner, Nikolaus 130
PHH Europe plc 112
Phillips, Bernard 32
Philpot, Graham 35
Pinehurst 58
Pinkertons Café-Bar 137

Pinnell, Alice and Anne 94
Pitt family 91
Plattes, Gabriel 30
Plummer, Thomas 93
Plummer, Richard 103
Plummer, William 101, 103
polytych 64
Ponting, Mr and Mrs 111
Porsche 149
Potter, John 130
Prinnells, The 15, 30, 55, 96
Prinnels 55
Priory Vale 14
Purkis, Alfred Leonard 94
Purton 9, 11, 13, 16, 20, 25, 34, 57, 83, 98
Putnam, David 54

Quadrant, The 57

Radnor Street Cemetery 91
Ram Leaze 93
Ramleaze 15, 19, 29–30, 54
Ray, River 9, 13, 41, 47–9
Ray, River, Parkway 48
Read, Max 58
Rebbeck, William Alfred, and family 102–4
Red Oaks Primary School 146
Redcap Gardens 30
Reedy, Carlyle 62
Reid's Piece, Purton 34
Renault Building 118, 120, 125; see also Spectrum Building
Ridgeway Farm 15–6, 21, 25, 32
Ridgeway School, Wroughton 19
Rivera, Edenia 62
Rivermead 49, 134
Rochester, Earl of 31
Rodbourne 13
Rome 131
Roughmoor 11, 16, 19, 131
Roughmoor Farm 96-8
Roughmoor Way 25, 106
Row Moor 96
Rowton Heath Way 27
RSK Group 123
Ruby, Morgana 54
Rugama, Marco 62
Rumming, William J 88

Russian maps 22
RWE npower 69, 112
Rycote Close 29

Sacof, D H 28
Sadler, Thomas, and family 101, 103
St John family 31, 63-8, 74-5, 77-8, 80, 83, 103; see also Bolingbroke
Salt Way Primary School 19–20, 59, 141, 151
Sandys-Renton, Tim 54
Sasson, Michael 116
Savage, Ken 54, 135
Sayer, Jo 49
Shaftesbury, Earls of, and family 97–8
Shannells, The, and Far Shannells 87
Shaw 9, 15, 19, 25, 28, 30, 39, 44, 83, 95, 104-7, 117, 126
Shaw Farm 45, 99, 103; see also Lower and upper Shaw Farms
Shaw Forest Park (Community Forest) 45-8
Shaw House 105
Shaw Residents Association 15-16
Shaw Ridge 14-15, 19-21, 35, 41, 44, 126
Shaw Ridge Leisure Park 55, 115, 127, 135-6
Shaw Ridge Primary School 38, 59–60, 141, 143, 151
Shaw Street 111
Shelfinch, Great 93
Sheppard, Libbie 98
Sherry, Ken 125
Shetland Close 30
Shortgrove Wood 65
Shropshire 80
Shropshire Light Infantry 111
Slade, Casey 133
Sleaford Close 74
Smith, Bryan 135
Smith, David 89
Sparcells 15–6, 48, 97–8
Sparcells Drive 25
Spectrum Building 118–20; see also Renault Building
Spencer, Lady Diana 31
Spencer Close 31, 55
Stamford Bridge, battle 27

Stamford Close 27
Standard Housing Co 28
Stemp, Adrian 116
Stoke Wake (Dorset) 131
Stonefield Close 104
Stonehenge 52
Stonehill Green 57
Stratton St Margaret 13
Stroud 131
Sudeley Castle (Glos) 29
Sudeley Way 29
Sutton, Thomas 86
Swansea School of Art (Institute of Higher Education) 55, 125
Swindon *passim*
Swinley Drive 98

Taiwan 131
Tarzan Trail 60
Taylor Wimpey 16
Tewkesbury, battle 26
Tewkesbury Way 26, 85, 126
Thames, River 41
Thames Water 48
Thamesdown Borough 20–1, 25, 28, 48, 50, 88, 96, 113, 125, 129, 131–2, 135, 152
Thornhill Hundred 84
Thunderbird totem pole 60
Tomkins, Oliver, school 18, 85, 151
Toot and Whistle pub (Toothill Tavern) 116-17, 121
Toothill 9–10, 14, 17–8, 22, 25–7, 32–3, 39, 48, 51, 53, 55–6, 82–3, 85, 121–2, 124–5
Toothill church 130
Toothill Community Centre 55, 124
Toothill Farm 32, 82, 86, 88-90, 92
Toothill Primary School 116-17, 144, 151
Trigonos 112
Tuckey family 86, 99–100, 104–5
Tumpy, field 93
Turnham Green 38
Turnpike Road 85
Tweed, George, gardens 118

Uffington (Oxon) 52
Unity Garden 142

Upper Shaw Farm 18, 32, 44, 82, 96, 101-4

Vodafone 141
Volvo 85

Wakefield, battle 27
Wakefield Close 27
Waldershare (Kent) 63
Walmart 115
Warneford School, Highworth 146
Washpool 106
Water Research Centre (WRc) 123
Waters, Terry 98
Welby, Rev Justin (archbishop of Canterbury) 77
Welsh School of Architectural Glass 56
Welton Road 134
Wessex 35
Wessex Taverns 116
West Swindon *passim*
Westlea 14–5, 18–9, 21–2, 39, 49–52, 57–9, 102, 134, 150–1
Westlea Campus 21, 146, 147
Westlea Down 27-8
Westlea Fire Station 147
Westlea Park 51, 151
Westlea Primary School 58-9, 85, 137
Westmead Drive 39
Westwords, poem 7, 150–1
Whitbread Flowers (Severn Inns) 120, 122
Whitehill 33, 86, 92
Whitehill Farm 33, 92
Whitehill Way 26, 30, 87, 92
Whitmore, Magaret 78
Whitmore, William 80
Wichelstowe 48
Wild Duckmead 11
Wilmot, John 31
Wilmot Close 31
Wimpey 15; *see also* Taylor Wimpey
Windmill, The, pub 120, 122
Windmill Hill 35, 112
Windmill Hill Business Park 87-8, 108-9, 111
Windmill Hill Primary School 19-20, 85
Windmill Leaze Farm 67
Winlaw, William 30
Winrow, Sarah 58

Winstone, Charles John 102
Wintle, Richard 50, 54, 68, 72, 77, 134, 144
Withy Bed 89
Woolford, Elliot 83
Wootton Bassett 83–4
Wootton Bassett Road 24, 88
Worlidge Drive 52
Worsley Road 38

WRc (Water Research Centre) 123
Wroughton 19, 35, 84, 86, 91
Wyk, de, family 94
Wyvern Architects 131

Yorke, Jasper 89
Yorkshire 26

Zeppelin Building 140

Hobnob Press

Hobnob Press has published more than twenty books about Swindon, and our list of titles about Wiltshire and the surrounding region runs into hundreds. Our Swindon books may be purchased from Swindon Central Library and from local booksellers. Or you can browse our catalogue and order directly from our website: **www.hobnobpress.co.uk**. If you have enjoyed this book you are sure to like its companion volume, **Swindon Decoded: the curious history of a remarkable town**, by John Chandler, as well as works by two of its authors, **The Ladies of Lydiard**, by Frances Bevan, and **Swindon, a Born Again Swindonian's Guide**, by Angela Atkinson. Also very relevant are **The Archaeology of the Borough of Swindon**, by Bernard Phillips, and two invaluable reference books by Mark Child, **The Swindon Book**, and **The Swindon Book Companion**. These and all our titles are described in detail on our website.

www.hobnobpress.co.uk

Milton Keynes UK
Ingram Content Group UK Ltd.
UKHW050235011123
431615UK00013B/14